You Can Always Judge a Book by the Company it Keeps.

Read What These Enthusiastic People are Saying:

"This book is packed with empowering and inspirational success strategies to help students build the future they want after college."
—**Jack Canfield,** Co-creator, *Chicken Soup for the Soul®* series; author of the bestseller, *The Success Principles*

"The networking system in this book is powerful. It has helped me build relationships that have not only benefited me professionally but personally, academically and emotionally as well."
—**Kristal Young,** Student, Harvard University

"This book will open your eyes to how exploring your passion can work with the knowledge and skills you gain in college to give you the edge you need in a competitive job market and lay the foundation for the career of your dreams."
—**Judith Harrison,** Senior Vice President of Human Resources, Ruder Finn Worldwide

"As a student, the most important thing to discover is a career you will be passionate about. This book has an exceptional system for showing you exactly how to do it!"
—**Rudy Ruettiger,** inspiration for the blockbuster movie *Rudy*

"I loved the financial advice in this book. Students who apply these concepts will be set for life."
—**T. Harv Eker,** Author of the #1 *New York Times* bestseller, *Secrets of the Millionaire Mind*

"If you want to learn how to meet people who will land you jobs, make you money and support you in launching your career, then read this book! It is packed with master networking techniques that will be useful for you right now—a must-read!"

—**Jill Lublin**, Author, *Networking Magic* and radio host of *Do the Dream*

"The strategies contained within the pages of this book are extremely practical and are similar to the ones I used in school, in business and on *The Apprentice*. These young men are truly extraordinary, and this is a must-have for anyone enrolled in an institution of higher learning!"

—**Nick Warnock**, Finalist on *The Apprentice*, season one

"A powerful book that not only inspires students but also enables them to take positive action towards a fulfilling future."

—**John Hufnagel**, Offensive Coordinator, New York Giants

"Don't think a degree and a good GPA will cut it—it won't! Read this book to find out the new approach that will make college the best investment of your life!"

—**Robert Allen**, Author of the bestseller, *Multiple Streams of Income;* co-author, *Cracking the Millionaire Code*

"By applying 2 of the principles from this book I discovered my dream job and have raised half a million to produce my first movie."

—**David Tal**, Graduate, UCLA

"To make being a college student effortless and easy, read *The Power of Focus for College Students*."

—**Mark Victor Hansen**, Co-creator, *Chicken Soup for the Soul®* series; author, *The One-Minute Millionaire*

"The financial advice in this book is some of the best content I've seen on how to create financial freedom. For those who want to control their financial destiny, this book is simply a must-have. I have already gotten started."

—**Ike Mbanefo**, Student, Duke University

"Formal education will make you a living, self-education will make you a fortune. Devour this book now, so you can enjoy all of the good fortune that life has to offer in the future."

—**Jim Rohn**, America's foremost business philosopher

"The secret to living and finishing rich is starting smart. *The Power of Focus for College Students* is a smart-start program that everyone will enjoy."

—**David Bach**, Author of the #1 *New York Times* bestseller, *The Automatic Millionaire* and *Start Late, Finish Rich*

"It was the principles of this book that helped me land a job as an investment banker on Wall Street right out of college."

—**Dave Dobrowolski**, Graduate, Ivey School of Business, University of Western Ontario

"Andrew and Luc are to college success what Wayne Gretzky is to hockey. If their book doesn't do it for ya, then not much will."

—**Jared Aulin**, NHL hockey player, Washington Capitals

"More and more students are enrolling at my university with their major as 'undeclared.' They do not know why they are in college and wander around wasting their time and talents. This powerful, insightful book is a winner for all college students, but especially for those determining their life direction. I plan to use it in my Honor's class, Personal Excellence."

—**William Bailey**, Ph.D., Associate Professor, University of Arkansas

"If you could be given a roadmap to success in college and in life, this book would be it. It helps the reader define what their ultimate career is, then takes them through a simple process that leads them to the treasure. A must-read by any student who feels lost in the woods."

—**Gary Tuerack**, President, The National Society of Leadership & Success; author, *Better Grades in Less Time*

"The goal setting system in *The Power of Focus for College Students* is awesome! I now have a clear plan that keeps me motivated and focused on the achievements that are most important to me."
—**Bryce Henson**, Student, Michigan State University

"I wish I had read this sort of book a generation ago when I went to college. However, the information contained in this book is far more important today than it ever was."
—**Pat Williams**, Senior Vice President, Orlando Magic

"If you grab hold of these focusing strategies now, you can avoid many of the pitfalls that adults fall into later, including jobs they don't enjoy and serious financial pressure."
—**Patricia Fripp**, Past-President of the National Speakers Association; Executive Speech Coach

"I've had the privilege of meeting thousands of college students over the last decade and can't think of two better role models for students to learn from than Andrew Hewitt and Luc d'Abadie. They are true dreamers!"
—**Eric Lochtefeld**, President and Founder, University of Dreams

"The Passion Puzzle™ instantly gave me clarity and direction. I never knew something so simple and fun could be life changing."
—**Kristen Brodhead**, Student, University of Texas

"This is a fun, insightful, unique guide that will propel college students into their best future! Every student needs one!"
—**Dr. Charlie Self**, Ph.D, M.A., Professor, Bethany College; pastor of Adult Ministries, Bethel Church

"This book should be a requirement for undergraduates! The skills and principles this book sets in place will not only make your college career successful, but sets you up with the life skills you need upon graduation."
—**Samantha Zipp**, Director, Membership and Marketing, University of Arizona

"Spending four years and at least $50,000 to get a degree is only half of what you need to succeed. This book will show you the other half. I wish someone would have given it to me before I started college, it would have been a real shortcut to success."
—**Sam Beckford**, President, Successful Studio Strategies; author, *The Small Business Millionaire*

"WOW! What a book! With the fast-paced, high tech and always changing Information Age we live in, a new approach to college is needed. *The Power of Focus for College Students* will show you step-by-step the right approach."
—**Aaron "The Enthusiator" Davis**, Author, speaker and member of the '94 University of Nebraska championship football team

"The Passion Puzzle™ opened my eyes to career options I had previously ignored. I am now considering entrepreneurship over a corporate atmosphere and feel so much more confident in my future career path."
—**Meagan Kempen**, Student, University of Wisconsin-La Crosse

"If I'd had this book when I was just getting started, I would have been financially independent 10 years sooner."
—**Don R. Campbell**, President, Real Estate Investment Network; author of the bestseller, *Real Estate Investing in Canada*

"Andrew and Luc are among the most impressive twenty-somethings I have ever met. They are going to change the world."
—**Patrick Combs**, Speaker and author of the bestseller, *Major in Success*

"Despite the modern mystique, it is possible to graduate from college or university with no debt and savings in the bank. I have two children who have already done it. They used many of the principles and techniques that you'll find in this book."
—**Henry Zondervan**, Principal, Foundations for the Future Charter Academy

"As a parent of two teenagers and an educator with 20 years of experience, I can say that the experienced-focused mindset suggested in this book has the power to transform your child's learning experience in college."
—**Deborah H. Streeter**, Sr. Professor of Personal Enterprise and Small Business Management, Cornell University

"By using the ideas in this book, I stepped outside my comfort zone and traveled to 10 countries, all through cool college programs."
—**Allie Ketcham**, Student, McGill University

"If you are in college or even a recent graduate buy this book immediately!!! It is an amazing guide for young people—full to the brim with inspiring yet practical ideas for soaring to new heights of personal and professional achievement."
—**David McNally**, Author of the bestseller, *Even Eagles Need a Push*

"This book will show you how to set goals effectively and how to articulate them clearly so your opportunities for success after college are maximized."
—**Burt Nadler**, Assistant Dean and Career Center Director, University of Rochester; author, *The Everything Resume Book*

"If you are worried about your child wasting thousands of dollars and not getting much out of their college degree—this book is an absolute must-read."
—**Mike Walsh**, President, High Performers International

"To be a top performer in the NHL, in business or in college requires commitment and tremendous focus. This book shows you how!"
—**Kelly Hrudey**, Former NHL All-star, Hockey Night In Canada analyst

"The fear fighting strategies in this book gave me the courage to change my major and go after the career I really wanted. Every student from freshmen to senior should own a copy of *The Power of Focus for College Students!*"
—**Brianne Webb**, Student, University of Oklahoma

"*The Power of Focus for College Students* is not a must-read—it is a must-read over and over again! I worked for a Canadian Embassy overseas, taught English in rural China, was President of the university Academic Mentorship Committee, and am now engaged in graduate work at Cambridge University—all thanks to the great advice in this book!"

—**Rob Alarie**, Masters Student, Cambridge University

"The purpose of college is to help us get the job we dream about instead of just the job that is left over. *The Power of Focus for College Students* shows you how. It works for college students, teenagers and everyone else who desires to get their adult life off to a great start!"

—**Dan Clark**, CSP, CPAE, Speaker, Co-author, *Chicken Soup for the College Soul*

"This is the most valuable book a college student could own!"

—**Vince Poscente**, Olympic athlete; author, *Leadership for the Self, The Ant and The Elephant*

"Students often 'lack focus' simply because they don't know what to focus on. This book will empower students to focus on what matters most—finding a career that they will be passionate about and how to kick start that career."

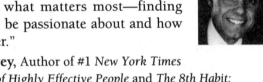

—**Dr. Stephen R. Covey**, Author of #1 *New York Times* bestseller, *The 7 Habits of Highly Effective People* and *The 8th Habit: From Effectiveness to Greatness*

"Andrew Hewitt and Luc d'Abadie have done a masterful job of combining their respective modern personal college experiences with old fashioned commonsense to create a practical and thought provoking book. *The Power of Focus for College Students* will no doubt provide significant guidance and wisdom to young people."

—**Glen N. Huber**, President & Founder, Chrysalis Capital Advisors Inc., Strategic Business Advisor and Investment Banker

The Power of FOCUS

for COLLEGE STUDENTS

**Les Hewitt
Andrew Hewitt
Luc d'Abadie**

**Health Communications, Inc.
Deerfield Beach, Florida**

www.hcibooks.com

To preserve confidentiality, various names have been changed in this manuscript.

Library of Congress Cataloging-in-Publication Data

Hewitt, Les.
    Power of focus for college students: how to make college the best investment of your life. / Les Hewitt, Andrew Hewitt, Luc d'Abadie.
      p. cm.
    ISBN-13: 978-0-7573-0289-3
    ISBN-10: 0-7573-0289-0
    I to be filled in here—General. II. Hewitt, Les. IIII. Hewitt, Andrew.
IV. d'Abadie, Luc. V. Title

© 2006 Health Communications, Inc.

Publisher: Health Communications, Inc.
           3201 S.W. 15th Street
           Deerfield Beach, FL 33442-8190

Cover Design and inside Text Design /Layout
Ghaile Pocock, Bulldog Communication Inc. (403) 228-9861.

Cover "eyes" Model
Josh Bietz

Cover Photographer
Chris Keating, C.N.C. Photography (403) 245-4897
www.cncphotography.com

Cartoon Illustrator
Casey Johnson, www.demoncamp.com

Les

To anyone who is about to enter college or university:

No matter where you've come from or what your
current status is, take this golden opportunity
to build a solid foundation for a future that is rich in
knowledge, passion and financial freedom.

Andrew

To Mom & Dad:

Thanks for giving me the roots to grow strong,
the wings to fly high and the freedom
to make mistakes.

Luc

To Joanna & Dre:

Without you, I would have never maximized
my college experience.

ACKNOWLEDGMENTS

This book was written from all corners of the continent, from a train traversing the prairies of Canada to the beach in California to a skyscraper in New York. It has been an eventful journey that wouldn't have been possible without the tremendous talent and support of several individuals. Glasses in the air to our team:

To Les Hewitt, co-author and mentor; if there is one person we could not have done without, it would definitely be Les. Your wisdom, guidance and writing expertise have made this manuscript what it is.

To *The Power of Focus* editing team: Our senior editor, Rod Chapman, whose expertise molded the manuscript into its most palatable form, and his wife Jennifer, who made sure the proofreading was thorough and accurate under tight timelines.

Big thanks to Ghaile Pocock who designed the cover and did the design/layout of the inside text. Ghaile created the look for *The Power of Focus* book series and has worked on all four series titles. Cheers to our talented photographer Chris Keating for the great bio and cover shots, and to the cover model, Josh Bietz— looking sharp! We are still in awe of our amazing cartoon illustrator, Casey Johnson, who magically put ideas into pictures. We appreciated the efforts of Georgina Forrest for coordinating the Reader's Panel and making our lives more organized. Our sincerest thanks to our readers panel and all of the individuals who helped test this content—Sam Zipp, Penny Giovanetto, Charlie & Michael Self, Jevan Pollo, Tyler Hayden, Arvind Chaudhary, Sophie Huterstein, Nicole Henson, Jenna Moeller, Dane Sutherland, Anna Trenouth, Stephanie Crisanti, Claire Daly, Patty Wagner, Nicki & Lyndsay Heikkinen, Burt Nadler, and Heather Ramsay. You guys rock!

The support team at The Power of Focus, Inc. was magnificent. Hats off to Jean Romain, Valerie Hindley, Ben Gumienny and especially Lynn Moerschbacher for her valued assistance.

A really big thank you to Fran Hewitt, who allowed us to transform two bedrooms of her home into a war zone, which became the hub of creativity. Your support (and dinners) kept us refueled throughout the entire project.

To our publisher, Health Communications, Inc., for their ongoing support and diligence, especially Peter Vegso, Allison Janse, Kim Weiss, Bret Witter and Lori Golden.

A big thank you to Donald Trump for believing in the message of this book and for educating and entertaining us on Thursday evenings with *The Apprentice*—our favorite reason for taking a break. To Michael Sexton, President of Trump University, for his valuable support and assistance.

We are grateful to: Patrick Combs for being a great friend, and mentor; Eric Lochtefeld and the University of Dreams crew for helping us follow our dreams; James Burgin, Jon Ward and Carolita Oliveros for supporting our big thinking and always being willing to help. Many thanks also to Jack Canfield, Sam Beckford and Dan Clark for their continued guidance.

To the many others who acted as a pillar of support, an answer to an urgent question, a contributor of a story, a critic for a cartoon or just a boost of positive energy when it was needed. Hats off to Mike Daciw, Andre d'Abadie, Adam Mysliwy, Kevin Ablett, Gavin Turnbull, Jennifer Gumienny, Janet Vielguth, Jackie Luff, Joanna Duong, Burt Nadler, Peter Bielagus, Gavin Radzick, Jared Aulin, Tyler Irving, Don Campbell, Cara Moeller, Pasquale Greco, Graeme Melton, Charlie Caudill, Ben Barry, Mike Costache, Darren Weeks, Chris Barrett, Dr. Jerry Gray, Heather Ilsley, Donna Messer, Dan Kazakoff, Glenn Huber, Chris McKenzie, Greg Habstritt, Maureen Bennie, Gary Tuerack, Ellen Pyzik and Keith Cunningham.

Last but not least, we cannot forget to mention all of the students on the fringe of this adventure who consciously or inadvertently provided insight and support.

CONTENTS

FOCUSING STRATEGY #9
Summiting The Mountain 252
Your journey to true satisfaction and fulfillment.

F O R E W O R D

BY D O N A L D   J .   T R U M P

 I'm someone who takes education seriously, and so do the authors of this book. Education should never be underestimated. It is a foundation, and foundations matter. I also know the importance of focus when it comes to any endeavor. Without focus, even diligent efforts can leave you without results. I call this striving without thriving. What's the point of that?

That's just one of the many very good points made in this book. The authors make it clear it's a lot better to thrive, not just survive, during and after your college career. This intelligent choice can be made by you when you decide to focus on what you're doing. You'll also learn why this is an important skill to acquire and hone. Focusing on your goals will serve you well for the rest of your life. I can testify to that.

Don't learn the hard way, which is often the too late way. Invest your time wisely now by reading this book. It's been well researched and presents the facts in a succinct and easy-to-grasp way. The writers have focused on their material and it shows.

Powerful people are focused people. Focus on this book and give yourself a head start.

See you at the top,

Donald J. Trump

Donald J. Trump

Why are the vast majority of college students struggling over what career to pursue . . .

then struggling even more to find a decent job?

Dear student (or browsing parent):

There's a disturbing phenomenon that is affecting young people in greater numbers every year. It's simply this: more and more graduates remain jobless or become stuck in unfulfilling careers. The statistics tell the tale. More than one in five college graduates remain unemployed six months after being released into the real world. Scarier still, research shows that more than 70 percent of graduates are dissatisfied with their careers within the first five years.

> What are the remaining 30 percent of satisfied students—the successful ones—doing that the others are not?

That's what this book is all about. By applying the phenomenally successful *Power of Focus* principles to college life, we've discovered a unique formula for success. It's all about learning to focus and follow through. And more importantly, discovering what you want to focus on. Unfortunately, this formula is not taught within classroom walls, and very few students are aware of it. Thanks to the new Information Age, the route to success in college is different now than it was 25 years ago. The traditional approach—get a degree with good grades from a respected school—isn't enough anymore. Employers want more than someone with a degree willing to fill a job. Also, graduates themselves want a fulfilling career, not just a paycheck.

Although college is a fantastic opportunity to prepare for a bright future, obtaining a degree is only a small component of what's needed for success in the real world. A second degree may seem like the easy answer. But it's not that simple. What's really required is much more encompassing.

So what *is* the solution?

Between us we have invested 11 years in college life, searching for the answer to that question. In addition to obtaining our respective degrees, we read piles of personal development books, conducted research, spoke to hundreds of college students and thoroughly tested our findings. We determined the top challenges students face (and we also experienced them firsthand):

- struggling to decide which career to pursue
- not knowing the best ways to gain the skills and experience employers want
- scrambling to manage money issues
- being swamped with assignments and deadlines
- facing inexperience on how to build personal and professional relationships
- battling procrastination and fear
- competing to find meaningful work after graduation

We went through many trials and tons of errors until finally uncovering what worked . . . and it worked **phenomenally well!**

The solution is to develop what we call the **experience-focused mindset** and apply **timeless success principles** not taught in college. You, too, can discover how to develop an experience-focused mindset and learn these timeless success principles by simply reading the nine focusing strategies in this book.

Our fellow author, Les Hewitt, brings an additional dimension to the table. In addition to being Andrew's father, he is the creator of the bestselling series *The Power of Focus* and is one of North America's top business coaches. With over 20 years of experience in the personal development industry, Les has helped thousands of clients reach outstanding success personally, professionally and financially. His insights will help you expand these focusing strategies far beyond your college experience. By teaming up, we have compressed the most powerful success principles of our time into the following pages—translated into student lingo, applied to college life and presented in a style that is fun to read and easy to implement. The result is a simple guide that shares, in practical terms, what it takes to make college the best investment of your life!

Tried, tested and true—how it worked for us

When we first started college, we thought the best way to ensure future success was by maintaining an honor roll standing while pursuing a degree at a reputable school.

We were dead wrong!

After using this approach for two years, we still weren't clear about what career to pursue or what we were truly passionate about. We were clueless about how to build relationships, how to ask for what we wanted, how to overcome procrastination and fear, or how to manage money. We were teenagers moving blindly into the real adult world with uncertainty and dissatisfaction coming at us full tilt. We were sitting in the dark, frustrated! This frustration finally led to a revolution in our mindset. We realized that in order to create a better future for ourselves—which is the #1 reason you go to college in the first place—we had to change our game plans.

We began to see college as a land of opportunity where we could gain valuable life experience, instead of an institution that would present us with a glorified piece of paper. The next three years told a much different story. Our new approach led to unprecedented personal successes, amazing experiences and nationwide recognition. We determined what careers fascinated us, met hundreds of like-minded students, and began to get recruited by some of the biggest companies in the nation. In addition, we learned how to lead, manage conflict, communicate effectively, act decisively and build lasting relationships—skills that employers wanted.

Between us we traveled to over 50 cities across 22 countries—all through cool college programs—living in culturally diverse settings from London, England, to Utrecht, Holland, as well as Los Angeles, Toronto and Kuala Lumpur, Malaysia. We participated in dozens of intercollege conferences and competitions, won various awards and scholarships, and ended up being featured in newspapers, prominent magazines, and even on billboards. Our network of friends, professionals and business contacts swelled into the thousands. We remain in touch with many of those people, and they continue to open doors we couldn't open on our own. We became mentors to many fellow students, and we were asked to participate as Dream Discovery Coaches for students accepted into the exclusive University of Dreams program. Opportunities continued to come our way and we created a plan for an exciting career (which has since unfolded into a prosperous venture). In the end, college turned out to be one helluva investment!

We'll show you how to do it, too, one step at a time. You'll find the payoff is incredible—one that will yield huge results so you, too, can create the future you truly desire.

It saddened us (still does) to see so many students spending thousands of dollars on tuition fees and graduating with hollow hopes instead of concrete opportunities. Most have never discovered the winning mindset and the skills needed for success after college. The majority are still lost, and many are jobless. For these students college wasn't the investment it could have been, or they thought it would be.

"Leap of faith."

During our research we found very few books or resources that taught students the successful strategies we started using. This book is a product of our drive and mission to make a difference in the lives of students. It is our commitment and guarantee that this book will equip you with the knowledge and tools necessary for making college the absolute best investment you'll ever make, bar none.

Our dream is for these success principles to be taught to every student who steps foot on a college campus. Every student should have the opportunity to pursue their dreams with passion and purpose, instead of being stuck in a job that all too quickly becomes boring and unfulfilling. Don't you agree?

Benefits! Benefits! BENEFITS!

Do you want clarity on what career direction is best for you? Do you want to discover how students secure jobs with top-rated companies months *before* they graduate? Helping you determine and pursue your ultimate career is only the start of what this book is all about. You will also discover:

- a proven method to achieve financial freedom and how money *really* works

- how to overcome the two biggest roadblocks that prevent you from getting what you desire

- a three-step process for turning any chance encounter into a valuable contact

- a simple formula for transforming bad habits into new successful ones

- what 3 percent of Yale students do that lead them to more success and bigger bank accounts than the other 97 percent combined

That's not all. You will also learn:

- how to tap into your true life purpose and live your dream

- a simple activity that will uncover your true passions

- a powerful job hunting method with a success rate proven to be 21 times more effective than online applications and 12 times more effective than applying with a resume

Who will get the most out of this book?

This book is for high school students, college freshmen, college sophomores, college juniors and seniors, and veteran students pursuing advanced degrees. It will also help students in any major—from fine arts to entrepreneurship to engineering.

Caution!

The Power of Focus for College Students is <u>NOT</u> a book with tips and tricks on how to survive college.

We do not focus on how to survive anything. We don't want you to merely survive, we want you to *thrive*! This book goes beyond study tips, resume writing and cafeteria food.

It focuses on helping you build a solid foundation so you can find and pursue the career of your dreams.

Not many students know these principles, and those who do are among the 30 percent who love their jobs and have reached outstanding levels of success. Implementing what you learn in this book will make you a member of this elite group.

Making it work for you

You will get way more from actually reading this book than by putting it under your pillow and attempting to learn through osmosis. Trust us on that one! Keep a pen with you when you read. Why? To scribble notes in the margins, circle or highlight key points, and **most importantly** to complete the Action Steps at the end of each focusing strategy. These are the stepping-stones that give you the opportunity to take what you've learned and convert it into ACTION! This is where the real learning takes place. If you want to truly harness these principles and have BIG results, then the Action Steps are a must.

The Focus Zone @ www.focusedstudent.com

To make the Action Steps more interactive and enjoyable, we have created online versions which can be found in *The Focus Zone* at *www.focusedstudent.com*.

As an owner of this book, you will have access to *The Focus Zone* and its treasure chest of free information, gifts and goodies that will help accelerate your progress. Keep your eyes peeled for the treasure chest logo as you read—you won't want to miss the bonuses inside.

Get FREE Access! Get your pass-code now by sending an email to: register@focusedstudent.com. Don't forget to include the ISBN number of the book (see back cover) in the subject line. By registering, you will receive your first free gift (a $30 value)!

College is a massive investment of your time and money. For most students it is more than four years of their life with an average cost of almost $60,000 in tuition alone. Unless you just inherited a fortune, you probably care about how well this time and money is spent. Implementing the focusing strategies in this book will not only make college a good investment, it will make college the best investment of your life. So let's get started—the countdown to your graduation has already begun!

To your success,

Making College Count in the 21st Century

A lot of fellows nowadays have a B.A., M.B.A., or Ph.D. Unfortunately, they don't have a J.O.B.

—Fats Domino

Let's tell it like it is. You can either go through the motions of college and end up with a degree, or you can maximize your college experience and end up with an abundance of cool career opportunities doing something you will love. The reality is, most students just go through the motions, defaulting into one of three postgraduate scenarios. The following are real-life examples.

NAME: Teresa Martin   SCHOOL: University of Texas, Austin

DEGREE: Psychology   DEBT: $0

STATUS: Working at a local sports bar in Austin and still living at home. Has been working part-time since her junior year, and this evolved into a full-time position after graduation seven months ago. Under pressure from her parents, she is considering going back to school to study law.

(Teresa Martin *continued.*)

FRUSTRATION: Although Teresa doesn't mind working at the bar, it isn't where she pictured herself ending up. Her parents, after paying the big tuition bills at a reputable college, are naturally disappointed. They wish she was applying her degree, pursuing a more attractive career and living independently.

Constant pressure from her parents is driving Teresa up the wall. She simply doesn't know what career she wants to pursue and is struggling to find a way to apply her degree. She wishes she had put more thought into this and explored her options in greater depth while in college. Applications are due for law school in a few months, but she is paralyzed with indecision.

NAME: Taylor Smith   SCHOOL: New York University

DEGREE: Finance   DEBT: $67,000

STATUS: Working as a securities analyst for a large bank in New York. With a serious girlfriend and 18 months in a stable career, he is well-settled into postcollege life.

FRUSTRATION: Although successful in the eyes of his friends and family, Taylor has great disdain for the career path he chose. Long hours and routine work are wearing him down, leaving him with little energy for himself and his girlfriend. He now realizes that the image of the finance field he carried through school was candy-coated by the high salary and prestige.

Taylor wishes he had pursued something he was truly interested in and excited about—sports broadcasting perhaps, or journalism. With growing expenses and a seemingly inescapable debt load, Taylor feels stuck. He would love nothing more than to be able to go back to college and do it all over again.

NAME: Steven Lee   SCHOOL: Colorado State University

DEGREE: Comp. Sci.   DEBT: $31,000

STATUS: Finished school eight and a half months ago and is still unemployed. Sent out more than 120 resumes, yielding only two interviews with no callbacks. Now spends the majority of his days playing computer games. Has basically given up on the job search, having recovered from the shock of realizing there was no corner office waiting for him upon graduation.

FRUSTRATION: He knows he has the skills to excel in a variety of information technology jobs and is deeply frustrated about not being able to get his foot in the door. He blames the economy, but knows there is more to the equation. As the weeks drift by with no job in sight, his self-confidence and self-worth continue to plummet. The only thing getting better is his computer game scores.

What's wrong with these pictures? Why didn't those thousands of tuition dollars propel Teresa, Taylor and Steven into more fulfilling futures? Sadly, Teresa, Taylor and Steven are only three of the millions of college graduates who each year fit similar profiles.

A great many of us drift through college hoping that life will work out later, hoping that the degree we earn will be a ticket to a successful and fulfilling future. In the last century this approach may have worked. Now, however, things are much different. In this first focusing strategy you will learn a new approach to college. Adopting this new approach is an essential step in making college the rewarding investment it should be. By putting these concepts into action, you will begin discovering what career you really want to pursue and start developing experience that will make you invaluable to employers. Best of all, college will become less stressful and a lot more fun. But first we owe you an explanation on why this new approach is so badly needed.

The Information
AGE

The Information Age has taken the world by storm. The black-and-white televisions, typewriters and snail mail that our parents grew up with have been replaced by plasma TVs, cell phones and the Internet. Think for a minute—what would this week be like if you didn't have a cell phone or an Internet connection? Weird, isn't it?

The Information Age has changed the way the world operates. Global borders have become almost invisible, competition has soared both locally and internationally, the pace of life has picked up speed, and keeping up with technology has become as hopeless as chasing a Ferrari Testarosa in a Ford Tempo. Buying purses to match shoes has evolved to include matching cell phone face plates and top-40 ring tones. Also, kids in Malaysia now bob their heads to Jay-Z and buy chromed-out rims for their mopeds.

Let's take a look at what else has changed since the disco days of the '70s:

- In the '70s there were less than 800,000 college graduates per year; today this number has more than tripled to 2.4 million.

- In the '70s the average 38-year-old had changed jobs 4 times; today the average number of jobs is up to 10!

- Since the '70s, more than 1,000 new colleges have sprouted up across the country.

- Since the '70s, the number of 26-year-olds living with their parents has almost doubled.

In this age of information we have more of everything—400 channels on the TV, 10 different flavors of Coke, more life opportunities, more available jobs and more job shopping. The times of stability and predictability that our grey-haired parents lived through have morphed into a fast-paced flurry of information and innovation.

"Sorry to get you out of school this early, son,
but I need your help with this computer."

This new era is different in another significant way. Distinctions alone are not enough. The value you offer a company is less and less dependent on what degree you have and what college you attend. Companies want people who can think outside the box, identify their own strengths and weaknesses, work well in teams, adapt to change, and communicate effectively . . . and that's just the start. Aspiring artists and ambitious entrepreneurs also need these skills to succeed and survive in this new world.

What Employers Want:
Getting Hired in the Information Age

"It's not the pedigree—the school, degree or GPA—that is important. It's what the person brings to the table. Internship experience, extracurricular activities and sheer enthusiasm for the job are what I consider the most important."

–Judith Harrison, Senior Vice President of Human Resources,
  Ruder Finn Worldwide

"Employers want focused individuals who know what they want and who can clearly state goals in field-focused terms."

–Burt Nadler, College Career Services Professional, author of
  The Everything Resume Book and The Everything Cover Letter Book

"The students who impress us the most are those who have shown real passion and delivery in some field of their life. They may have led a team on the sports field, changed lives through a community project or increased sales in a part-time job. The actual activity is less important than the energy and enthusiasm they put into it."

–Linda Emery, Head of Recruitment, Unilever UK

This new era has not only changed the needs and desires of companies, it has changed the needs and desires of individuals as well. People want more because they see that more is possible. Opportunities and knowledge are no longer dependent on social status, family name or material wealth. Today, people want more out of life than a safe and secure job. On average, people will change jobs 10 times to seek work that is more fulfilling. The pursuit of wealth, quality of life and Louis Vuitton accessories is widespread and achievable by anyone with a strong enough drive.

The World Has
CHANGED

Life was much different in the Great Depression of the 1930s—workers were laid off in droves, businesses closed their doors, and those who could find work were few and far between. Jobs were almost impossible to come by and so were cheesy accident lawyers. Job security was a rare luxury. Basic survival was the focus. But after the Depression and World War II the economy took flight, creating an explosion of jobs and a phenomenon known as the Baby Boom. The workforce demanded more skilled labor, and as a result more colleges were built to train people to become everything from doctors and lawyers to engineers and accountants.

As the hippies and peace signs of the 1960s turned into the disco jockeys and afros of the '70s, college enrollment continued to soar. In the decade between 1970 and 1980, college enrollment shot up 31 percent. By the year 2000, over three million more students were enrolled in North American colleges than there were in 1980. The prestige of a college degree was being diluted by the day.

The times, they are a changin'.

—Bob Dylan

The education system has not changed. Once upon a time, college was a means to an end. The system worked like a well-oiled machine, where the world needed workers trained in specific skills and colleges were the places that trained students to fill this need. For the most part, baby boomers were more than happy to accept the jobs for which their college education had prepared them. Most stayed in these jobs for the majority of their working lives. The world has since changed—people want more and employers want more—but the education system has stayed pretty much the same. The gap between the demands of the world and the offerings of the education system continues to widen.

> *The most dangerous way to approach college is with the idea that all you need to do is pay your dues and get your degree.*

> —Patrick Combs

Few colleges have programs and courses that help students determine what field of study best fits their talents. Nor do they teach them the life skills needed to excel in this competitive environment or encourage them to pursue their dreams in this new age of opportunity. A dangerous scenario has been created. Students who approach college with the same mentality as their parents or grandparents are preparing themselves for a world that no longer exists—leaving them unable to capture the plentiful opportunities available.

College Success in the INFORMATION AGE

The good news is that college can still be an incredible investment—arguably the best investment of your life. However, to make college a good investment in the Information Age, one change is critical—a change in mindset. You can have one of two mindsets toward college: a *degree-focused* mindset or an *experience-focused* mindset.

The Degree-focused Mindset

This is the traditional way of thinking, passed down through generations. This mindset is founded on the belief that *degree qualifications* are the ticket to a promising career and a bright future.

How to Recognize the Degree–focused Mindset	
SAY THINGS LIKE . . .	ARE KNOWN TO . . .
"Getting involved in school activities and clubs is a waste of time."	Compete with their class-mates and constantly dispute their grades.
"I hear that Art 202 is a guaranteed A!"	Take two majors to increase the prestige of their degree.
"I'm studying to be an accountant because there are a lot of accounting jobs available."	Take additional courses or study in the summer so they can get their degree sooner.
"I just want to be finished with school . . ."	Do the minimum required courses so they can finish as fast as possible.

Most students start college with a degree-focused mindset. If this is the mindset you currently have, don't sweat it. It isn't your fault.

This mindset has been passed down from your parents' generation because it was the mindset in their time. Some students have a change of mindset during college, but many never make the transition at all.

Three Misconceptions of the Degree-focused Mindset

SELECTING YOUR MAJOR IS A PRIORITY

About 75 percent of students will change their major at least once during college and, according to career expert David Swanson, 75 percent of jobs are filled by people without the proper degree qualifications. That means only 25 percent of people actually work in the field they studied in college. Don't sweat your major.

YOUR GRADES ARE WHAT MATTER MOST

Yes, grades are important. You need to meet minimum levels so they don't kick you out, and if you choose to go to graduate school you may need a certain average to get in. Cassandra McCarthy, a highest GPA award winner from Edinboro University says, "As exciting as it was, my award for the highest GPA has done little for me. What continues to bring the most opportunities my way are the extracurricular activities I was involved in, the people I met and the real-world experience I gained."

A survey conducted by Stanford University in 2003 found that GPA was ranked 11th on a top-20 list of what employers look for when hiring. The top three were communication skills, integrity and interpersonal skills.

FINISHING FASTER IS BETTER

College is the best place to make mistakes. Use your college days to determine what career you want to pursue. You can get qualified people to help you without being invoiced for their time. You can also participate in internship programs, international exchanges and a variety of events that will help you discover an ideal career. You can build connections and experience that will help get your foot in the door. When you rush to finish in four years, you limit the number of experiences you can have. However, be warned—when you start receiving more invitations to weddings than keg parties, it's time to move on.

The Experience-focused Mindset

The experience-focused mindset didn't exist a few decades ago—it didn't need to. Students with this mindset anticipate that the *experience* they gain in college will contribute most to accelerating their careers. By experience we mean much more than work experience—we are referring to the college experience as a whole.

Experience-focused students want more than an 8½-by-11-inch piece of paper in a fancy gold frame—they want to determine their interests, improve their skill set, build a network of valuable contacts, create opportunities for themselves after graduation and have fun at the same time. They look at college as a window of opportunity. To them, college is not a means to an end; it's a journey of discovery and development. They don't rely on their degree alone to showcase their credibility. Instead, they differentiate themselves from the pack through the experiences they seek out, and through the knowledge and skills they learn along the way.

"English lit—how about you?"

How to Recognize the Experience-focused Mindset

SAY THINGS LIKE . . .	ARE KNOWN TO . . .
"I'm running for a VP position on the student government."	Volunteer for several events, clubs and activities.
"I hear you can learn a lot in Public Speaking 101!"	Have multiple groups of friends and contacts.
"I chose to major in architectural design because I have always been interested in it."	Take fewer classes to free up time for extracurricular activities.
"I don't mind taking an extra year to finish."	Change majors, spend a year working and/or studying abroad.
"I only get one shot at college. I better make the most of it."	Seek out internships to develop new skills and clarity on career interests.

ANDREW:

The university I attended had one of the most innovative programs in the nation. It had won several awards for excellence and had received rave reviews from student participants. The course prided itself on putting theory into practice—using case studies and community projects as teaching tools, rather than overbearing text books and boring professors. It came time to make a decision. Do I participate in this highly regarded, award-winning program and enhance my experience or do I double-major and increase the prestige of my degree? At the time, I was inebriated by the degree-focused mindset—taking more classes than I could handle and guarding my GPA from any courses that could be a threat.

The grades and the degree won me over. I pansied out. I was more concerned about what my degree would say on it than what I was learning in the process. By the end of the year my poor decision was painfully obvious. More than half of the students in this innovative program were selected to compete in the country's most prestigious case competition.

To make a long story short, they ended up dominating the competition. They were flown across the country on an all-expenses-paid trip, featured in magazines, newspapers and on TV, and after it was over they had numerous employment opportunities. Do you think I had regrets? You better believe it! It was the second-worst decision I had ever made in college (second to a not-so-inconspicuous attempt to relocate a vending machine to my dorm room).

Maximizing Your Return
ON INVESTMENT

Investing in college is much like investing in the stock market. Your investment approach depends on market conditions and your desired rate of return. Market conditions of the Industrial Age favored workers who were trained in specific skills—the return on investment students desired was a safe and secure job. The degree-focused mindset was the investment approach that best met these market conditions.

But what are market conditions like today? An interesting phenomenon is taking the world by storm . . .

College Investors be Warned

A new demographic has surfaced that is continuing to grow in greater numbers every year—not only in North America, but across the world.

This demographic has caught the eye of the media and been assigned interesting labels:

Boomerang Kids: young adults who 'return to the nest' after graduating from college. (*CBS News, Canada*)

Twixters: 20-somethings who are 'betwixt and between' adolescence and adulthood. *(TIME magazine, USA)*

KIPPERS: A British acronym for Kids In Parent's Pockets Eroding Retirement Savings. (*BBC News, UK*)

Evidence Exa

The victims who wear these labels are the struggling college grads whose college education didn't pave the way into promising futures, as they had hoped. Twentysomethings Inc. found that 64 percent of college grads move back in with their parents —a percentage that has nearly doubled since the 1970s and is continuing to rise each year.

Parents feeling squeezed by rising tuition fees are growing frustrated with their children's struggle to become self-sufficient after graduation. They don't understand why a college degree isn't leading to good opportunities, like it did back in their day.

Graduates are also frustrated. Their expectations of life after graduation are being crushed by not landing a job or not knowing what they want to do. The longer they live at home, unemployed or working at meaningless jobs, the more their confidence and motivation erodes, thus compounding the problem.

College investors everywhere are frustrated with the market conditions and the new phenomenon that is taking place.

Interestingly, in the midst of the current volatile market, some students are managing to make college an amazing investment. They clarify what career they want to pursue, develop the real-world skills employers want, are recognized for their involvement, meet tons of interesting people and thoroughly enjoy college life. These students have discovered the investment approach that works best today. What investment approach are they using? You guessed it—the experience-focused mindset. This mindset allows you to discover the real-life skills you can combine with your academic learning so you can walk out of college into a career full of opportunities . . . and avoid having to move back in with your parents. Students who adopt an experience-focused mindset are the most savvy investors. Not surprisingly, they are earning the greatest returns.

According to the National Center for Education Statistics (NCES), the average cost of an undergraduate college education is just shy of $60,000. How you approach this investment is your choice. If you want to become a savvy investor, we recommend you read the next section carefully. You will learn what only a small percentage of successful students know—how to use the experience-focused mindset to make college the best investment of your life!

The Experience-focused
FORMULA

Those who approach college with an experience-focused mindset will see a playground of opportunities before them. From internship programs and international exchanges to extracurricular activities and innovative degree programs—college offers a variety of fun and invaluable opportunities. You can discover what careers interest you most, build life-long friendships and gain experience that will guide you along the path to success.

ANDREW:

It wasn't until halfway through my sophomore year that I had my first glimpse of an experience-focused mindset. I attended a five-day student business conference in the Rocky Mountains of Jasper, Alberta. At the conference I met a different breed of student—a breed I hadn't seen before. They had a different outlook on college and did more than just study (which at the time was my compulsion). They ran student clubs, organized student events, attended conferences and had a good understanding of what they wanted to do upon graduation—not to mention they were having the time of their lives!

What also intrigued me was the fan club of corporate recruiters present at this conference. They paid a lot of attention to these proactive students. By the end of the conference my mindset toward college had done a complete 180. I realized that college had more to offer than boring books and long lectures, and that it was involvement in these events that impressed companies. These students were learning real-world skills. The day after I returned from the conference I applied for an executive position with a club on campus. By the time I graduated I was club president, had started a variety of new events, programs and clubs, attended more than 15 student conferences nationwide, and had been recruited by over half a dozen companies. This simple change in mindset literally changed my life.

Ready to learn the magic formula? Here we go . . . . The experience-focused formula contains the following key components:

International Exchanges + Internships and
Co-op Programs + Extracurricular Activities +
Innovative Courses and Programs =

The Experience-focused Formula

---

1. International Exchanges

Getting sick of your campus scenery? Thinking it's time you made a trip to a beautiful tropical beach with mesmerizing white sand and crystal clear water? Imagine you could get course credit for doing such a thing... you can! Believe it or not, every college student is capable of doing an international exchange to destinations as far north as the Canadian Rockies or as far south as the Australian Outback. It's a pretty cool setup—you fill a seat at a college overseas and in exchange an international student fills your seat at your home college. In addition to studying abroad, programs exist that allow you to work abroad in an international setting. You might be thinking: "My GPA isn't high enough to be eligible for these," or "My faculty doesn't offer these types of programs." Even if your college doesn't offer an exchange program or has a long list of bureaucratic criteria that could prevent you from being eligible, you can still go!

Treasure #1, your first free gift, awaits you at *The Focus Zone*. Go to *www.focusedstudent.com* to receive "Exchange Your Life—eight ways to study or work anywhere in the world."

ANDREW:

With my new experience-focused mindset I became an eager beaver, looking to take advantage of every interesting experience my university offered. I decided to go on the "five-year program" and extend my studies to allow enough time for an exchange program . . . or two . . . or three. A year and a half later I had gone on three different international exchanges, visited more than 12 countries and could mimic the airline safety instructions.

My experiences abroad were nothing short of AMAZING—the most enriching experiences of my life. Words cannot describe how much I learned, not only about other cultures but about myself as well. Exploring tropical islands and shopping in exotic markets wasn't too shabby either.

Many benefits come with studying abroad:

- You gain real-life experiences that can't be learned from a textbook, no matter how overpriced or overweight.

- You demonstrate to employers that you have experience adjusting to unfamiliar circumstances and handling unpredictable problems—traits needed in this new era of rapid change.

- You'll meet new friends from across the globe—it's always nice to have a place to stay when the travel bug hits you.

- You'll acquire interesting stories and memories to last a lifetime—yup, expect to be sharing travel tales with your kids.

2. Internships and Co-op Programs

According to a study done by Northwestern University, these two exciting opportunities—internships and co-op programs—have a 64 percent chance of landing you a full-time job. So what are they exactly? Internships are short-term jobs that are unpaid and offer you experience in an industry of interest. You can find internship opportunities through school programs, or by contacting companies directly or searching online. Co-op jobs also offer real-world work experience but are usually longer term, paid and offer course credit. To gain access to co-op opportunities look for a co-op programs office on your campus.

LUC:
When it was time to apply for college, my strategy was to look through magazines and Ivy-league listings for the most reputable schools. I figured that the better the school, the more valuable my degree, and the more plentiful the job opportunities would be. A few weeks before I started my college application blitz, I was at my

aunt's house for dinner and met Todd, a well-dressed guy in his late twenties who had an attractive girlfriend and drove a flashy sports car. I instantly admired the guy, or should I say I admired his lifestyle. Over the course of the evening Todd recommended that I go to a school with a great co-op program—not surprisingly, he highly recommended the university he had attended. He ranted and raved about how important work experience was, and not the degree.

A few weeks later when I started the application process to all the high-profile schools, I added co-op programs to my list of criteria (now I had two). A few months later, to my delight, I received acceptance from all the reputable schools I had applied to, but I was most excited when I got accepted into the school with the best co-op program in the nation—the school Todd had recommended. It didn't take me long to choose which offer I was going to accept. Although I didn't know it at the time, I had taken my first step in the direction of the experience-focused mindset.

In addition to the future hook-ups that internships and co-op jobs offer, they also provide fantastic opportunities to discover your interests and determine what type of work you enjoy. It's kind of like shopping for clothes—before you commit to a purchase you get to try on different sizes and styles until you find the perfect fit. Your college (or its career center) is like the shopping center; it has a selection of good jobs to choose from, and it ensures they meet specific standards.

By enrolling in an internship or co-op program you save search time, gain great experience and develop a better understanding of what type of career is a good fit for you. They also are a ticket to working at some of the coolest and most cutting-edge companies around. When it comes to finding a summer job, check out these opportunities—it's hard to go wrong.

LUC:

During my second co-op term at the height of the dot-com era, I decided to jump on the bandwagon and get into Information Technology. I spent four months bored and frustrated as a programmer. I used to gaze out at the marketing department across the hall, dreaming I could be on the other side. When I got my review at the end of the co-op placement it read, "Luc is a hard-working employee, but not cut out for IT and should consider something different. Overall rating: Satisfactory." Satisfactory was the lowest possible rating and really was a synonym for *you suck!*

My next co-op term I got a marketing job and absolutely loved it. Not to mention I got a much better review and the highest possible rating—Outstanding. It's chilling for me to even imagine working as an IT programmer full-time. I'm glad I tested the waters before diving in.

Some amazing internship and co-op programs are largely unknown and not specific to any college—all students can apply. These programs give every student an opportunity to land a dream job in Hollywood, or to work in a skyscraper in New York City, or to help staff one of the most advanced research facilities on earth.

Treasure #2 in *The Focus Zone* at *www.focusedstudent.com* contains a comprehensive list of the coolest internship programs on the planet. Check 'em out to make your job search exciting rather than exasperating.

3. Extracurricular Activities

Extracurricular activities can include things like clubs, conferences, sports teams, fraternities and sororities. If you have survived the first week of college, you have likely been bombarded by these organizations begging you to sign up for an event, join their club or brand yourself with their apparel. It's easy to turn a cheek to these sometimes overbearing volunteers, pick out faults in their organization or make excuses why you don't have time to get involved. Retreating to your next class is the easy and painless solution. As a result, many students overlook and miss out on the HUGE benefits these extracurricular activities offer. The best thing to do is to join something that interests you. If necessary, persuade a friend to join as well.

ANDREW:
In high school I thought I was too cool for school. I avoided extracurricular activities and student councils like the plague and hung around with the "tough crowd" to try to sustain a cool-kid image. College was a much-needed wake-up call. Employers weren't going to care how big the subwoofers were in my buddy's car or how crazy my friend's cousin was. Employers cared about practical experience. Volunteering and student clubs ended up being my ticket to a much cooler future.

If you are interested in marketing, you might join a student association like a marketing club or an advertising society. This is a tremendous start for taking advantage of extracurricular activities. If you want to take your experience to the next level, there is another type of association you can join that is arguably the best and quickest way to network with people in the industry, remain up-to-date on the latest trends, meet people working in your dream job and add killer lines to your resume. Over 90 percent of students don't know about these associations, and for that exact reason they are your opportunity to really stand out from your peers.

These are called . . . (drum roll, please) . . . professional associations! So, if you want to "go pro" then join a professional association that meets your interests. Everything from the American Marketing Association to the Video Game Developers Association exists—there are literally thousands to choose from. Flick through the *Encyclopedia of Associations* at your local library or do a search online for professional association lists.

Traveling the Nation on a Shoestring Budget

You might have caught wind of a little something called conferences. Typically weekend events organized by student clubs, they are usually focused on a specific topic and include well-known speakers, entertaining events, four-course meals, hotel accommodations, and nightly parties. Students from across the country are invited, and travel fees are often subsidized by your school or covered by corporate sponsors. Attendees get to meet like-minded students and mingle with recruiters from the nation's largest companies. In short, these events are action-packed with amazing experiences and a lot of fun!

THE CATCH

To be in the know about these conferences and sometimes to be eligible to attend, you need to be involved with student organizations.

Here are a few of the benefits of extracurricular activities:

- Differentiate your resume by adding impressive lines like "Coordinated budgeting and event logistics for a fundraiser hosting over 400 students and university faculty," or "Managed a team of 12 executives responsible for five committees and a $150,000 budget."

- Meet students with similar interests and ambitions.

- Improve your communication/interpersonal skills.

- Get first dibs on cool events like listening to famous speakers, hosting wine and cheese gatherings for corporate recruiters, BBQs, attending all-expenses paid conferences across the nation, attending sporting events and intercollege parties (to name a few).

- Gain leadership and teamwork experience that employers and grad schools are looking for.

- Make a positive difference on campus and in the community by putting your ideas and skills to the test.

4. Innovative Courses and Programs

Are you fed up reading boring textbooks for the sole purpose of regurgitating the information you memorize on the next exam—only to forget 90 percent of it a few weeks later? Sadly, this situation can't always be avoided, but it can be offset with innovative courses and programs. Most colleges have started to realize the void in the system and are now implementing education alternatives that involve hands-on learning through projects, real-world applications or educational competitions.

These might take up more time in your schedule or involve additional effort to get enrolled, but in the end you will learn far more, enjoy the process more, develop greater experience and better retain the information. In addition, these programs often lead to prize money, free trips, job offers and nationwide exposure. These innovative programs, classes and competitions exist on all college campuses; however, many can also be found off-campus.

Benefits of Innovative Courses and Programs

"Being a child of the theatre, I was excited to get accepted into the Trinity College La Mama Program. It took me to New York City to study the performing arts for an entire semester. I got to see over 60 different performances, work at a well-known theater and meet some of the most accomplished performers in the city. At the end of the semester my supervisor offered me a full-time job. I haven't stopped smiling or dancing since."

–Jill Weinstein, Trinity College

Courses and Programs (*continued*)

"Having an entrepreneurial spirit, a class called New Venture Analysis caught my eye. In this course we developed a business plan then competed with the plan against other students from all over the world. We ended up winning over $70,000 in cash and prizes, and twice qualified to enter the Super Bowl of business plan competitions—Moot Corp—where we won best-written plan. Our success at these competitions attracted over a quarter of a million dollars in seed capital, allowing us to turn this school project into a full-time business. This class was the foundation of my entrepreneurial future."

–Kevin Michaluk, I.H. Asper School of Business, University of Manitoba

"The best course I ever took didn't have boring lectures or a daunting textbook. We had one assignment for the entire semester: to create a full-fledged PR campaign on the topic of education and ethics. For the second half of the course we competed against schools from across the country and ended up with an honourable mention from the Public Relations Society of America. I learned more in this course than I did in my entire freshman year. More importantly, I discovered that I loved PR and that it was the career I wanted to pursue. The following summer I landed a job in New York working for one of the largest PR firms in the world. The lady who interviewed me happened to be a judge from the competition. Taking this innovative course definitely paid off."

–Jaci Herbst, University of Wisconsin-Madison

Treasure #3 in *The Focus Zone* contains a top-10 list of the coolest college courses and competitions worth their weight in gold. Go to *The Focus Zone* at www.focusedstudent.com to find out what they are.

There you have it—the four key components of the experience-focused formula: International Exchanges + Internships and

Co-op Programs + Extracurricular Activities + Innovative Courses and Programs. But even after learning about these exciting opportunities many students still don't pursue them. This happens for two reasons—time and fear. Participating in these experiences requires reallocating time away from your daily study routine. It may also require pushing back your graduation date. Students who use the time excuse usually feel that high grades are a better option for securing a good job after college. Unfortunately, this assumption is false.

The second reason students shy away from the experience-focused formula is due to fear and a lack of confidence. Electing to participate in these experiences, and taking the initiative to get involved, often requires that you JUMP out of your comfort zone. The next section will show you how to do this easily.

Step Outside Your
COMFORT ZONE

"The eagle gently coaxed her offspring toward the edge of the nest. 'Why does the thrill of soaring have to begin with the fear of failing?' she thought. As in the tradition of the species, her nest was located high on the shelf of a sheer rock face. Below there was nothing but air to support the wings of each child. 'Is it possible it might not work?' she thought. Despite her fears, the eagle knew it was time. Until her children discovered their wings, there was no purpose for their lives. Until they learned how to soar, they would fail to understand the privilege it was to have been born an eagle. And so one by one she pushed them, and they flew!"

—Excerpts from *Even Eagles Need a Push,*
  David McNally

For baby eagles to spread their wings and fly, they have to leave the comfort of the nest. The nest is their comfort zone, a place where they feel safe, at ease and free from risk and fear.

Like baby eagles, we enjoy staying in our comfort zones. Why wouldn't we? It's more comfortable there. We talk to the same people in class, buy the same style of clothes, work at the same jobs and eat the same food. This placid existence is our comfort zone—our nest.

You miss all the shots you don't take.

—Wayne Gretzky

Are you happy with your current knowledge, accomplishments, experiences, friends and bank balance? Do you have absolutely no interest in growing as a person and in achieving new things? Not likely . . . or at least we hope not! You know that those who never take risks will never reap the potential rewards. Those who never visit unexplored territory will live boring lives. Those who do not challenge themselves will never grow wiser, and those who do not shoot will never score. To grow, you'll need to step outside your comfort zone into the area of uncertainty, risk and challenge. What would happen to the baby eagles if they never left the nest?

LUC:

When I moved away from home, my mom accompanied me on the cross-country trip to help me move into my anything-but-elegant dorm room. After three days she left—pushing me out of the nest. I stood alone in the parking lot waving to her as she drove away. It was two days before introduction week, and the school was deserted. I did a slow 360, examining the foreign environment. I didn't have my familiar car, I didn't have my trusted friends and now I didn't have my mom. I was 100 percent outside my comfort zone. Although I felt naked, I knew I had been

What Does Your Comfort Zone Feel Like?

Try this:

1. Fold your arms in front of you. Feel comfy? Natural and ordinary? Good. This is what your comfort zone feels like.

2. Now try folding your arms the other way—the opposite arm on top. Feel strange? Uncomfortable? This is what stepping outside of your comfort zone feels like.

pushed out of the nest and it was my time to fly!

What's cool is that the more experiences you take on, the more challenges you tackle, the more times you feel naked, the larger your comfort zone becomes. For example, after moving away from home you gradually become comfortable with the change and could do it again with ease—your comfort zone has stretched to include this new experience.

The more one does and sees and feels,
the more one is able to do.

—Amelia Earhart

Once stretched, it stays bigger. Constantly stretching your comfort zone moves you toward your full potential, gives you more experience to draw on and allows you to enjoy the many riches that life has to offer.

The experience-focused mindset gives you access to the finest opportunities college life offers, but you'll need to step out of your comfort zone to seize them. In the bigger life-picture, college is a brief window of time. It's easy to let it fly by, only to regret later that you didn't take advantage of the unlimited experiences and opportunities available to you as a student.

> *Ships in the harbor are safe, but that's*
> *not what ships are built for.*

—John A. Shedd

IT'S EASIER . . .

It's easier to settle for average than strive for excellence.

*It's easier to be saturated with complacency than
stirred with compassion.*

It's easier to be skeptical than successful.

It's easier to question than conquer.

*It's easier to rationalize your disappointments
than realize your dreams.*

It's easier to belch the baloney than bring home the bacon.

—Author Unknown

In college, it's easier to stay in your comfort zone than to step outside into the world of risk and uncertainty so you can grow and experience new things. What are you going to choose? Easy or experience—the choice is yours.

In the next chapter you'll discover the importance of finding your passion. You'll get to complete a puzzle that will help you define the best career choice for you, one that is totally in synch with what you love to do.

CONCLUSION

College can be the best investment of your life . . . but only if you maximize the experience.

Take Note—The World has Changed
- The wants of individuals and employers have increased, and for the most part the education system has stayed the same —a void has been created.

College Success in the Information Age
- People who have the degree-focused mindset anticipate that degree qualifications are the ticket to a promising career.
- People who have the experience-focused mindset anticipate that the experience they gain in college will contribute most in accelerating their careers.

The Experienced-focused Formula
- Work abroad or study abroad—or do both.
- Participate in extracurricular activities such as clubs, conferences, sports teams, frats and sororities, etc.
- Gain practical work experience through an internship or co-op program.
- Sign up for innovative courses and programs.

Step Outside Your Comfort Zone and into the World of Opportunity
- The world of new growth and opportunity always lies outside your comfort zone.
- Stretching your comfort zone accelerates your progress and gives you more experience to draw on.
- The experience-focused mindset requires that you step outside your comfort zone constantly.

Are you ready for the first round of Action Steps that will help you accomplish what you really want? They start now.

ACTION STEPS

Online version available in *The Focus Zone* at:
www.focusedstudent.com

The Experience-focused Formula

Expand Your Comfort Zone

The Experience-focused Formula

Write down the component of the experience-focused formula that appeals to you most. (Example: international exchange, extra-curriculars, internships and co-ops, or innovative programs.)

_____

Describe the specific experience you want to have using this component. (Example: going on an exchange to Paris, running for president of the geography club.)

_____

_____

_____

_____

What is one specific thing you can do this week that will move you closer to implementing the experience you described above?

_____

_____

(Write this in your calendar so you don't forget.)

Expand Your Comfort Zone

What is something you would like to do or feel you should do that will require you to step outside your comfort zone? (Example: ask a question in class, move away from home, go to a conference.)

_____

What are the benefits you will reap by taking action?

_____

_____

If you want the benefits above, describe what you will do to take action. Be specific. Include the date you will take action and the steps you will take.

_____

_____

_____

Ignite The Fire Within

The most powerful weapon on earth is the human soul on fire.

—Ferdinand Foch

Dahlia Lithwick seemed destined for success.
Her Yale education, Stanford law degree, a stint as a clerk in the 9th U.S. circuit appeals court and rising stardom within her law firm all pointed to a career filled with money and status. There was just one small glitch in the plan—she hated it.

At first, she didn't pay much attention to the rumblings of dissatisfaction. "I just thought the way my parents and everybody around them thought," Dahlia says. "Your job is supposed to suck. Happiness is something that happens between 9 A.M. Saturday and 10 P.M. Sunday."

Law had been a way to fill in the blank when faced with the question of what to do next. But, says Dahlia, "Law school was the three worst years of my life. I knew I had made a horrendous mistake but I didn't know how to undo it, or what I would do instead."

Years earlier, she had decided against being a writer— a career she deemed "narcissistic, silly, artistic and unprofessional." Yet she knew writing was an important piece of her identity. "I was one of those people who had kept a journal since I was 10. It was something I did the way other people breathed." But writing? As a living? Not surprisingly, a flood of negative images rushed into her brain. "Will I be wasting my college degree?" Dahlia remembers thinking. "What will my family think? How will I sleep at night knowing that I've wasted all this?" Finally, she looked at her writing and thought, "This is the one thing I know I love, beyond reason. To not at least try it seems crazy."

At 7 A.M. the next day Dahlia quit her job at the law firm and began writing a novel. "The idea of being in a financial and professional free fall scared me," she says now, looking back on her momentous decision. "But the really risky thing would have been to stay in a profession I hated. The risk was my health, and my relationships and my spiritual life continuing to decline indefinitely. Taking a year off and possibly living in poverty just didn't seem nearly as dangerous as being profoundly unhappy."

Dahlia struggled through her first year. Money was tight. However, she remained focused on making it work and sure enough, doors began to open. "I got a call from the online publication *Slate* saying, 'If you can be at the Microsoft trial tomorrow morning at nine o'clock, you can cover it for a couple of days.'" Dahlia delivered, and her talent didn't go unnoticed. Soon enough, *Slate* granted her a position as a full-time editor.

The rest of her story follows a similar tale. Her love for writing has continued to be a catalyst for her success. Dahlia is now the author of two books—*Me v. Everybody: Absurd Contracts for an Absurd World,* a legal humor book, and *I Will Sing Life: Voices from the Hole in the Wall Gang Camp.* Her work has appeared in the *New Republic, Commentary, the Washington Post, Elle,* CNN.com and *The New York Times.* "Everyone is entitled to soar," Dahlia smiles. "However, it is up to you to take the leap and find out what will make your wings flap."

Unlike some American Idols, this story is not a one-hit wonder. People who have passion for what they do, like Dahlia, continually rise to the top and achieve extraordinary things. A research study conducted by Dr. Srully Blotnick tracked 1,500 people for 20 years. Of the 1,500 people he studied, 83 percent had embarked on a career to make money, while only 17 percent had chosen a career based on what they loved to do. After 20 years, 101 of the 1,500 had become millionaires, and all but one of those millionaires were from the 17 percent who had chosen a career based on what they loved to do.

Here's another interesting statistic: according to the annual American Freshman Survey conducted by UCLA, 73.8 percent of students want to be "very well off" financially.

Now riddle me this, Batman: if almost three-quarters of the student population want to be wealthy, why are only 17 percent of students pursuing work they are passionate about?

Here are some startling statistics about how satisfied the workforce really is:

- 70 percent are unsatisfied with their current work.

- A survey by the Society for Human Resources Professionals found that 80 percent of the workforce would change jobs if a new job was available.

- Research done at the University of Maryland found that 70 percent of Americans earning over $30,000 a year said they would give up a day's pay each week for a day of free time, and 48 percent of Americans earning less than $20,000 a year said they would make the same deal—that is, trade part of their paycheck for more time off.

Why do the majority of people contribute to these saddening statistics? Why don't more people love what they do? The answer to these baffling questions can be found in the three critical concepts that follow—and they're not called critical concepts for nothin'. If you want to beat the odds and love what you do, brand these concepts into your consciousness.

The Power of
PASSION

Critical Concept #1—Passion is created, not discovered.

When it comes to passion, one of the biggest hiccups students have is trying to narrowly define what their passion is or what job they want. Have you been stressing yourself out not knowing what your passion is or what specific type of job you want? Don't sweat it! In spite of common terminology, no single thing is your passion. That's right, there isn't one thing that is your passion. Feel free to let out a sigh of relief, because you can stop searching. Here's how it works. Usually people connect passion to things they are really interested in. However, true passion goes beyond a deep interest—it's a powerful emotion. To create this emotion four ingredients are needed: values, interests, skills and ambitions. A career that can ignite a passion in you is a career that:

1. aligns with what you **value**
2. is in line with your **interests**
3. uses your **skills**
4. supports your **ambitions**

These four ingredients act like a fuel that, when applied to your work, combusts into an enthusiastic flame. The more fuel you throw on the fire (the more your values, interests, skills and ambitions are applied through your work), the larger the flame will be (the more passion your work will give you). An easy way to remember these four all-important ingredients is the word VISA (Values, Interests, Skills, Ambitions). Think of VISA as your passport to passion. Just as all of your personal data is required for a travel visa to be valid, your values, interests, skills and ambitions must work together to fully ignite your passion. Taking one ingredient out will drastically dilute the effect.

Can you see the good news here? Many different types of work can give you passion. You don't need to stress over finding your passion and narrowing your career search to one particular job. You can get passion from a variety of jobs in a variety of industries. As you uncover your values, interests, skills and ambitions, you will come to know your unique criteria for getting passion from your work. Ultimately, determining what career to choose and what jobs to apply for becomes much easier—you will know your criteria and have a checklist to evaluate your decisions. We'll show you how to do this a little bit later.

Critical Concept #2—Be passionate about the cause, not just the effect.

When you were young did you ever want to be a doctor so you could wear a stethoscope? Or be a circus performer so you could work with clowns? Do you still feel that way? Some still do.

ANDREW:

It was another boring day in my junior high career studies class, when out of the blue I had a compelling revelation. At the time I was a materialistic 13-year-old—the kind who only wore certain brand name clothes and only bought them if the brand name was clearly visible. I had developed a craving for expensive things and had determined that being wealthy was the only option for me. My teacher, Mr. Watson, was discussing different types of jobs in the medical field. I quickly perked up when the salary figures were introduced and became intrigued by one in particular—dentistry. My best friend's godfather is a dentist. It reminded me of all the cool stories I had heard about his new Porsche, fancy house, elite golf membership and the great seats he had to major sporting events. It didn't take much convincing. Actually, it didn't take ANY convincing. I was sold on the spot. I had found my ticket to the lifestyle I wanted—dentistry!

One year later I wasn't so convinced. Every week someone seemed to go out of their way to inform me that dentists had the highest suicide rate of any profession—it must have been on *Oprah* or something. Hearing this same demeaning statistic so many times really opened my eyes. Was it worth it? I was so caught up in finding a career that created the effect I wanted—the money, the cars, the big house—that I overlooked whether or not I would truly enjoy the work. I was fortunate to realize this when I did. For many, the realization comes too late.

This story illustrates how using the quickest method of getting the benefits you want is not an effective career planning strategy. When it comes to choosing a career, having an interest in the effect—money, lifestyle, status—shouldn't be your primary focus. You should also have a sincere interest in the cause—the type of work you will be doing on a day-to-day basis.

Why, you might ask? Consider the following: if you work eight hours each weekday you will be working for approximately 50 percent of your waking hours. By the time you add in commuting to and from work and menial chores such as running errands, washing dishes and doing laundry, the average person is left with only 20 percent of their time to do what he or she really wants. Working because you enjoy the cause ensures you enjoy the majority of your time on this planet, not just a fraction of it.

What can be even more mind-boggling is that even if you had all the money in the world and as much time as you wanted to enjoy it, satisfaction is *not* guaranteed. The most successful people prove that true enjoyment in life seldom comes from the effect of work—big house, fast car, fancy vacations. It comes from the cause—the work you do and the service you provide to others. John D. Rockefeller, no slouch in the achievement category, makes this telling observation: "I know of nothing more despicable and pathetic than a man who devotes all the hours of the waking day to the making of money for money's sake." Are you choosing a career for the effect? Or are you confident that you will enjoy the work that causes the effect?

Coincidence?

Highest income group in U.S.: **doctors**

Profession with highest proportion of
unhappy people: **doctors**

SOURCE: Jonathan Freedman in his book, *Happy People*

Here's a simple test to give you confidence that you are pursuing a career for the cause, not the effect. **Question: What aspect of your career choice most excites you?**

Take a moment to answer this question. If you are having a hard time, or if your answer is based solely on the effects the job produces (money, benefits, lifestyle, etc.) then think a little harder about whether this career is what you *really* want to do. On the other hand, if your answer relates to the work itself, you are on the right track.

Critical Concept #3—When you have passion, profits are not far away.

If you were to think of five very wealthy people, who would they be? Out of those five, how many love their work? Statistically, there is a 99 percent chance that all five have sheer passion for what they do. More interesting still, these wealthy people almost always choose to continue working despite the fact that they have acquired a fortune. Money isn't their motivator. Passion for their work keeps them going. Passion got them started, and passion allowed them to excel to where they are today. Think of Steve Irwin, the Crocodile Hunter. Do you think he would have risen to stardom if he wasn't passionate about wrestling crocs? Do you think Donald Trump would continue working 60-hour weeks if he wasn't passionate about real estate?

Fact or Fiction?

More heart attacks occur on Monday morning
than any other time during the week.

FACT: A 10-year study conducted by the *British Medical Journal* confirmed that five times more people die of heart attacks on Monday mornings than any other time during the week. Is it a coincidence that for many people Monday is the most-dreaded work day? We'll leave that for you to decide.

It can be difficult to pursue a passion and trust that it will pay off in the long run. Your parents may not approve and your friends might think you're crazy, but as the statistics show, when you choose to pursue something that will give you passion, the numbers end up in your favor.

However, it can be scary not knowing all the details! What type of work will you do? How will you get paid? Who will hire you? Where will you end up living? Will you have to wrestle crocodiles? To avoid this uncertainty and to reduce the chance of failure, most students follow the herd by choosing traditional jobs or careers—usually for the financial rewards. What they don't realize (and it isn't always obvious) is that pursuing something that ignites their passion is the best way to ensure long-term success. It also minimizes the chance of being led into a dissatisfying career that they don't realize until it's too late.

"Earl, if we pull this off we'll be heroes."

Having the required skills and a deep interest in your work is one heck of a competitive advantage! When you get passion from your work, work becomes energizing, empowering and easy. *Fortune* magazine discovered that highly motivated employees are 127 percent more productive. If you are not interested enough in your work to stay motivated, the people who are motivated will outperform you by 127 percent!

> *Without passion you don't have energy;*
> *without energy you have nothing.*

—Donald Trump

Passion gives you enthusiasm. Enthusiasm (which comes from the root word *God-powered*) gives you the fire to burn through anything. You can't burn through things until you find the fuel to light your fire within. Are you ready to find out what will ignite your fire?

What Ignites Your
FIRE?

This is the point where you either take action or you continue to stay in your safe, comfortable nest. Discovering what gives you passion requires that you look back on your past experiences and uncover your values, interests, skills and ambitions. It also requires that you continually strive to increase your understanding of these things as you progress through college.

Are you curious yet? Ready to discover what type of work will give you passion? Are you ready to kick-start your journey to ultimate satisfaction? Lace up your hiking boots—it's time to get started.

Before you begin the journey it's important to know that there are three levels of fulfillment—living with passion, living with purpose and living your dream. The rest of this chapter will focus on the first leg of the journey—living with passion. Discovering what will give you passion is the foundation of a fulfilling life and the path to realizing your purpose and dream. Your purpose and dream will be discussed in the final section of this book. As you progress through each level of fulfillment you reach a greater state of happiness, satisfaction and personal success.

Right now you may be immersed in the fog of the valley—uncertain about what lies ahead and unclear about the direction to choose. Picture yourself in this valley, surrounded by large mountains. Which one do you climb?

There is a mountain best suited to you; the trick is to determine which one it is before you get too high up the wrong mountain. The mountain that corresponds with your values, is in line with your interests, utilizes your skills and provides you with opportunities to reach your higher ambitions is the mountain you will climb the fastest.

Taking the time to determine what will give you passion is key in deciding which mountain is best for you. If you choose the wrong mountain—one that won't give you passion—your journey will be long, hard and tedious. You will be lacking the enthusiasm needed to keep you striding forward. Many students don't determine what gives them passion and soon find themselves halfway up the wrong mountain. If they are unwilling to turn back and start over again, they will secure a spot in the "I am unhappy with my job" club, living a far-from-fulfilling routine. In contrast, by discovering what will give you passion (by choosing the right mountain), your level of fulfillment will continue to grow. As your journey continues, the next levels of fulfillment will start coming into view.

Your time in the valley is representative of your time at college. During this time you have amazing opportunities to prepare for the exciting journey ahead, and to gain clarity about what direction to head in. Remember the experience-focused formula—international exchanges, internships and co-op programs, extracurricular activities, and innovative programs. These are the ultimate opportunities for gaining clarity and developing the abilities you will need.

Determining what gives you passion is like filling in a jigsaw puzzle. Your values, interests, skills and ambitions make up the puzzle. The pieces represent the things you know about yourself. The more pieces you put together, the clearer the picture becomes. The following section will cover each of the four components of passion in detail so you can start piecing together your very own Passion Puzzle™.

If you are interested in discovering work that will ignite you with passion, strap on your focusing hat and get ready to answer a few intriguing questions. This next activity—The Passion Puzzle™—will give you insight into your best career options. If you think you already know what career you want to pursue, this activity is a much-needed pit stop that will give you confidence of whether or not you are on the right track.

There are two ways to complete The Passion Puzzle™ activity. OPTION 1: Sharpen the ol' pencil, and as you read the next twelve pages, fill in the Passion Puzzle™ on page 64. OPTION 2: Go to *www.PassionPuzzle.com* and complete this activity online. It's also free and allows you to print a personal copy of your completed Puzzle. If you are determined to find a career you love, we highly recommend you check out *www.PassionPuzzle.com* and do this activity online.

The interactive online version includes examples and is easier to follow.

Piecing Together Your
PASSION PUZZLE ™

Here's how it works: the following pages contain several intriguing questions. Write the answers to these questions in the appropriate sections of your Passion Puzzle™ on page 64. Answering these questions will uncover your values, interests, skills and ambitions. The more questions you answer, the more complete your puzzle will be and the more clarity you will have about what careers will give you passion.

1. Determine your values

What do you value in a job, in a company, in a work setting and in your day-to-day life?

It is important that the career you pursue has the attributes you value. For example, if you value flexibility you may become frustrated, irritable or very unhappy if placed in a work environment that has rigid guidelines and procedures, despite how skilled or interested you are in the work. By clarifying what you value beforehand, it will be much easier for you to find jobs and eventually a career that suits you. Since determining what you value can be tough to do, we have included the most common values in the following chart.

Identify Your Values

creativity	flexibility	risk-taking	routine
adventure	high salary	human interaction	religion
low stress	prestige	advancement	authority
responsibility	freedom	recognition	privacy
team work	challenge	independence	travel
innovation	learning	helping others	control
predictability	stability	analytical thinking	balance
job security	integrity	wealth building	benefits

You might be thinking to yourself, "I value all of these things." You probably do, to some degree, but on which values do you place the most emphasis? Imagine that from the above list you could only choose five values. Which five would you choose? Add your top picks to the values section of your Passion Puzzle™ on page 64.

Think of past arguments or heated conversations you've had. Was something you value in jeopardy? Was someone compromising your freedom, your ability to be creative or your need to spend time with your family? What were you fighting to protect? (If you argue a lot, being heard might be something you value.) Don't lose these insights—add them to your Passion Puzzle™.

TIME OUT: Is determining what you value giving you a headache? Does it seem too challenging? Good news! Here are a few final questions (they're not tough, so don't worry) that will help you fill in all nine puzzle pieces in the values section of your Passion Puzzle™. Remember, values are what you value and what you value in a career. Check it out! If you are off-line, computer deprived or allergic to technology, the following questions will immediately help you fill in your puzzle.

Discover Your Values

What did your family value when you were young?
Did you always value the same things?
Which ones do you still value?

Think about past job descriptions you have read.
What in these descriptions excited you the most?

Think about a really cool job. What do you like about this job?
What makes it cool?

What is *really* important to you? What matters most?

If you could design the ultimate job, what attributes would it have?
Would you travel, earn a high salary, have lots of free time?

2. Determining your interests

Interests are things that capture your attention, keep you talking and fascinate you.

Your interests might include a sport or sports team, a type of technology, or a product. Maybe you are interested in a literary genre or magazine, a leisure activity or a hobby. Your interest could also be a form of art, a specific language, a subject in school or a field of study. Interests are plentiful, and they evolve as your preferences and experiences change. It makes sense that work you will be passionate about is work that is in line with your interests. Numerous studies show that the brain releases many endorphins when we speak of things we are interested in, and few or no endorphins when we speak of topics which we have little interest in. How does this tie into passion? The release of endorphins is a fundamental component of passion.

Endorphins increase your cognitive and reasoning ability, making you more alert, energetic and engaged—reducing your chances of falling asleep on the job, snoring in class or drooling on your keyboard.

A man is a success if he gets up in the
morning and goes to bed at night, and in
between does what he wants to do.

—Bob Dylan

We figure the same applies for women too—right, Bob?

ANDREW:
After two years at college I was still scratching my head, bewildered by career options and uncertain about what I really wanted to do. Being a compulsive planner, I couldn't stand the uncertainty. I had to take action. Two clicks of the mouse and I'd started a Word document that would have a profound impact on my life. I called it my *Skills & Interests Doc.*

I wrote down all the things I could think of that I was interested in or good at. It was hard at first, but as I continued through college this document continued to grow in size. I had unknowingly tuned into a powerful discovery process that helped me figure out what my skills and interests really were. Every time I felt a compelling interest or was conscious of having done something well, I captured the thought by writing it in my *Skills & Interests Doc.* It would have been nice to have a Passion Puzzle™ to fill in that was more encompassing and easier to use, but back then we hadn't developed it yet. Nonetheless, common trends started to appear. Over time, I developed clarity and confidence in what I was truly wired to do.

What if you could combine your interests with your work? Wouldn't that be an exciting way to live? Take time to ponder each of the questions below. Just one enlightened answer could spark a new idea, one that you'll be glad you discovered now, instead of 25 years later. Jot down your answers in the interests section of your Passion Puzzle™ on page 64.

Time Out: Are you writing your answers in the puzzle on page 64? We understand. Some people just don't like writing in books. If this is you, take advantage of the free online version at *www.PassionPuzzle.com.*

Discover Your Interests

Think about what your parents would say you really enjoyed doing as a child. Which of those childhood interests are still alive and well today?
What are your current favorite pastimes and hobbies? What would your favorite pastime be if you had time to learn and practice it?
Think about when time seems to fly by. What engages your interest so much that you lose track of time?
Visualize your bedroom, or, if you are already in it, look around. What signs of your interests do you see? (Beer posters, half-naked supermodels and movie hunks don't count.)
What subjects of conversation grab your attention and keep you talking until you get thirsty?
Think about the websites you visit frequently. What interests do these relate to? (if XXX sites are at the top of your list, photography may be a good option for you—joking!)
If you are shy, what topics of conversation bring you out of your shell?

3. Determining your skills

Skills include your natural talents and the abilities you have acquired. All in all, they are the things you do well.

When you use your skills, work becomes energizing, enjoyable and easy. Work that doesn't apply your skills leads to frustration and slows your progress.

The following animal school fable shows just how important acknowledging your skills really is:

Once upon a time a group of animals decided they would organize a school. They adopted an activity curriculum consisting of running, climbing, swimming and flying. To make it easier to administer the curriculum, each one of the animals took all four subjects.

The duck was excellent in swimming. But he made only passing grades in flying and was very poor in running. Since he was slow in running, he had to stay after school and drop swimming in order to practice running. This kept up until his webbed feet were badly worn and he ended up being average in swimming.

The rabbit started at the top of the class in running but had a nervous breakdown because he found swimming was incredibly hard work.

The squirrel was excellent in climbing until he developed frustration in the flying class because his teacher made him start from the ground up instead of from the treetop down. He also developed a charley horse from overexertion, and finished with a C in climbing and a D in running.

Moral: Don't make the animal school mistake of focusing on competencies you are average at. Focus on your brilliance, the things you excel at. Brilliance attracts big opportunities and big money.

> *A musician must make music, an artist must paint, a poet must write, if he is to be ultimately at peace with himself.*
>
> —Abraham Maslow

It's hard to focus on what you excel at—your skills—until you know what they are. Get that pencil ready. You are about to discover them . . .

Discover Your Skills   PART ONE

In the jobs you have worked, what skills did you demonstrate that impressed your employer? (Communication, teamwork, intrapersonal, analytical, etc.)

What talents and skills have you been recognized for? (Include compliments, awards, trophies, praise by your parents and teachers.)

Think about the subjects that were easiest for you in grade school. What skills do you have that allowed you to succeed in these subjects?

Think about the extracurricular activities you have excelled at (sports, dancing, singing, Scouts). What skills helped you succeed in these areas?

Think about the hobbies you really enjoy (cooking, craftwork, website design). What skill set do you use in these activities?

What roles did you play in your friendship groups? (Leader, communicator, organizer, caregiver, supporter, innovator, etc.)

Having a hard time thinking of specific skills? To stop drawing blanks, go to *www.PassionPuzzle.com* for a list of skills you can easily select from.

When you can pinpoint what you are skilled at, you can exercise the power of focus. By focusing on what you do best, you can attain excellence and become brilliant. Ducks should focus on swimming, rabbits should focus on running and squirrels should focus on climbing. What should you focus on?

Note: Do not skip past these questions! We know it takes time and effort, but the sooner you know what your skills are, the sooner you will know what courses, major and career you will excel at. Not determining your skills can leave you swimming upstream, going nowhere. Here are a few more questions to help you fill out the skill section of your puzzle.

Discover Your Skills	PART TWO
What would you say are your top three skills?	
Think about the courses you currently excel at. What skills do you have that are helping you excel at these courses?	
What do your friends say you are good at?	
Think about the things you're lousy at. Are there opposites of these weaknesses that you excel in?	
What do you do well that others find difficult?	
What do you do that causes others to marvel at your ability?	
What do you do effortlessly without a lot of preparation?	
What have you practiced over and over again that you are now highly skilled at?	

LUC:
When I first went to college I was like everyone else—
I randomly chose a major. My school was a leader in
computers and computer-related disciplines. It looked like
every second student was going to end up a programmer,
developer or in some career linked to technology. I jumped
in line with the rest of the freshmen and enrolled in a bunch
of computer science courses. I had been told I was good at
business and that I had an entrepreneurial tendency, but
I ignored it. My computer skills were mediocre at best, but I
focused on developing them further anyways, because that
was the hot ticket and everyone else was doing it. After a
couple of really low marks, put-you-to-sleep classes, mind-
numbing assignments and even a disastrous co-op term as
a junior programmer, I realized computers weren't for me.
I was swimming upstream. I then decided to switch my focus
to business, and in no time I had great marks, met great
people and was coasting with the current.

Are you coasting with the current? Or are you honing
skills that you are only average at? Don't let your environment or other people dictate what you should focus on.
The choice is always yours.

4. Determining your ambitions
Your ambitions are what you
want in the future—your wishes,
dreams and goals.

Thinking about them will excite,
inspire and motivate you. Ambitions can include making a certain
amount of money, running your
own business, being able to travel
around the world, becoming a
political leader, being on TV, being loved by children, becoming a celebrity, driving a fancy car, helping solve a world

epidemic, saving someone's life or inventing the next best thing since sliced bread. In other words, whatever gets you fired up. For you to be passionate about your work, you will always need to be striving for something bigger and better. These are your ambitions. This is the stuff dreams are made of—so think big! Obviously, some people are more ambitious than others. If you're on the less-ambitious side it's no big deal, just be sure to add a pinch of ambition—it is a necessary ingredient that will keep you motivated and passionate about your work.

Dan Clark was a stand-out athlete at the University of Utah. Dan was passionate about football. It was his most compelling interest, and he was one of the most highly skilled defensive ends in the nation. Dan's burning ambition was to carve out a successful career in the National Football League. He was so talented that the Los Angeles Raiders (now known as the Oakland Raiders) drafted him. The Raiders began grooming him to be a star who they hoped would lead them to a Super Bowl.

Sadly, it never happened. One day during practice Dan suffered a paralyzing injury that cut short his athletic career. Overnight, his football dreams were shattered.

Dan lost his identity. Football was what he did. What do you do when your ambitions have been snuffed out? Now, suddenly, he didn't know who he was anymore.

It wasn't easy, but almost by accident Dan's positive outlook opened up a new opportunity. He was invited to speak to a local high school football team, a team that was struggling in their division and in dire need of inspiration. Dan had little public speaking experience, but that didn't seem to matter. His speech made such an impact on his audience that they turned the season around and later became state champions.

The school board was impressed with Dan's performance, and to his surprise, after a few more local talks, he landed a contract to speak to 170 schools throughout Utah. During these speeches, Dan discovered a new talent and a new interest.

His football success had taught him the importance of thinking big, and now he began setting high ambitions for his unfolding speaking career. Today, Dan Clark is one of the most highly paid and in-demand professional speakers in the world. He has delivered speeches to more than 2.5 million people in 18 countries. His client list includes *Fortune* 500 companies, elite colleges, the U.S. Armed Forces, Super Bowl champions and even the United Nations World Congress.

Dan Clark found an alternative way to put his ambitions to use and to get passion from his work. He wanted to do big things. He didn't let an injury stop him from being passionate about his career and from making a positive impact on the world. Whether pursuing a career in football, public speaking or politics, don't forget about your ambitions. They are a fundamental component of passion and the ticket to big things. But first you need to know what your ambitions are. Get that pencil ready. It's time to fill in the last section of your Passion Puzzle™.

Discover Your Ambitions

What do you remember from your childhood daydreams that excited you?
What did you want to be when you grew up?
Think about the hopes and dreams your parents have for you. Are these in line with your own ambitions?
If a genie granted you three wishes, what would they be?
If you could have any job in the world, what (or whose) job would it be? What is it about this job that you like most?

Discover Your Ambitions *(continued)*

What would you do if you couldn't fail?
What would you do if you didn't need money?
What do you daydream about doing or becoming?
Write down three things that you *really* want, that energize you just thinking about them?
What are the three biggest accomplishments you want to achieve in your life?
Imagine you just visited a doctor who told you that you have only five years to live. What ambitions would you set out to fulfill in your time remaining?
Envision a perfect day 10 years from now. What does it look like?

Dig a Little Deeper . . . There are many excellent online assessments that will help you further clarify your values, interests, skills and ambitions and will recommend careers based on the results. Check out at least one, but don't skip these gold mines of wisdom. Best of all, a lot of them are free.

www.superherotraining.com
www.princetonreview.com/cte/quiz
www.careerkey.org
www.self-directed-search.com
www.analyzemycareer.com
www.kolbe.com
www.discoveryourpersonality.com
www.trumpuniversity.com/learn/selfAssessment.cfm

Harnessing The Power of
YOUR PUZZLE

••• DISCLAIMER •••

NOTE: The careers your Passion Puzzle™ point you toward may be completely out of line with what you are studying. This is common and shouldn't be a cause for concern.

REMEMBER TWO THINGS: First, you can always change majors—college is not a race. Second, 75 percent of people work in jobs unrelated to their degree qualifications, and this doesn't mean your degree is a waste.

What do you see?

After filling out your Passion Puzzle™ and staring at it like a hypnotized monkey, your mind might be buzzing with job and career ideas. Don't lose these thoughts. Write them down in Your Career Discovery List on page 66. Hold up your Passion Puzzle™ and stare at it once again.Throw away any preconceptions you have. Pretend this is the puzzle of a stranger and you are a detective who has been hired to uncover potential careers. On page 66, write down everything that comes to mind, regardless of whether or not you would pursue this line of work or think it's even possible. What careers or jobs could fulfill those values, appeal to those interests, use those skills and bring out those ambitions? Don't agonize trying to think of careers that utilize all the individual pieces of the puzzle—just make sure the four major sections are represented. You might be specific and write: *baseball news reporter, deep sea photographer or social worker for underprivileged children.*

If you are having a hard time thinking of specific careers or job titles (which is absolutely normal), then think of ideal job descriptions that utilize pieces from each of the four sections of your puzzle. You could write, *working in fashion—doing writing and teaching—flexible hours—recognition and prestige—potential to write a book.*

Come up with as many ideal job descriptions and career ideas as you can and add them to Your Career Discovery List on page 66. Anything goes, so don't restrict yourself to conventional titles and rules. Get creative and write down the unique and seemingly wacky ideas as well. Remember, anything that incorporates pieces from all four sections of your Passion Puzzle™ will ignite your fire within.

What do others see?
Some people have a knack for connecting things, some don't. If it isn't in your gene pool, find a gene pool that is good at it. Share your Passion Puzzle™ with others—people who know you well and people who don't know you well enough to have any bias in their answers. Ask them to put their detective hats on and investigate your puzzle, looking for clear con-nections that lead to career ideas or ideal job descriptions.Other people will see things you don't, and they will likelycome up with ideas that escaped you—creative types are partic-ularly good at this.

What do experts see?
Take your Passion Puzzle™ to your career counselor, to a career center or to someone else who is an expert in this field. These are the people who can help you match vague ideas with specific career and job titles. Every school has a career devel-opment center that will welcome you with open arms and applaud your initiative.

Use the free resources at *www.PassionPuzzle.com*
On this website, you will find examples of how others have used their Passion Puzzle to determine their dream career. If you're looking for more clarity on how to get the most out of your completed puzzle, definitely visit this website—*www.PassionPuzzle.com.*

Investigate Your
CAREER IDEAS

Okay, so you have an idea about jobs and careers that you will have passion for—excellent start. Now it's time to test the turf so you can be sure the career you have in mind is a great fit. The following three strategies will give you a sneak peek at the ins and outs of the career. As well, they have been proven to dramatically increase your chances of hearing the magic words, "You're hired!"

Informational Interviews
These differ from traditional interviews in two ways. First, you interview a company, instead of a company interviewing you. Second, you are seeking information, not direct employment. And, according to Richard Bolles, author of the best-selling job-hunting book in the world, *What Color is Your Parachute?*, people who use informational interviews have a 31 percent employment success rate compared to 4 percent who use resumes. Here is a simple four-step system for making informational interviews work for you.

Step 1: Determine Who You Want to Connect With
Find the e-mail address or phone number of a person in a leadership role who is working in the career field you want to investigate (preferably at a company you would love to work at). Be creative if necessary—information is always available to those who are creative about finding it.

Step 2: Make Contact and Set Up an Interview
Get in touch either through e-mail or over the phone and ask if you could treat the person to lunch or coffee to get advice and insights. If using e-mail, send a sincere (but not too long) e-mail explaining your curiosity for this line of work and

your interest in learning how the person became successful in the industry.

Step 3: The Informational Interview

Meet with this individual and get him or her talking with enthusiasm. Arrive prepared with a few key questions so you can steer the conversation and keep things moving. People like talking about themselves and giving advice to young ambitious types (you).

Give them the opportunity to share their successes and to share their passion for their work. A great question to get things started is, "Did you have any idea what career you wanted to pursue while you were in college? I'd love to get your advice on how you discovered [job title] was a good fit." You could also have the person recommend the values, interests, skills and ambitions they think someone should have for this career.

Step 4: Build the Relationship

If you find yourself sitting on the edge of your seat wishing you were the other person, focus on building the relationship further. You could ask questions like, "What are things I should be doing now?" "Are internships really the best way to get my foot in the door?" "Where should I look?"

Guess what may happen? If you play your cards right, there is a good chance they will recommend you intern at their company. Booya!

One caution with informational interviews: don't let it appear that your agenda is to get an internship or a job, because it shouldn't be. In an informational interview you should be genuinely seeking information—landing an internship opportunity is just a bonus, but a likely one. Another thing: although a career may sound amazing, just as the cafeteria special can sound delicious, until you actually experience the work or eat the meal you cannot be certain it is going to satisfy your appetite. That's what the next two strategies are for.

For a more in-depth review on how to make informational interviews work for you, go to *The Focus Zone* at *www.focusedstudent.com* and pick up Treasure #4. Students who follow the advice in this treasure consistently email us amazing stories of landing dream jobs and getting crystal clarity on their career direction.

Job Shadowing

Imagine it is 10 years from now and you are successful in your desired career. A friendly student (like you) calls up and asks if she can shadow you on the job for an afternoon. What would you say? If the student was genuinely interested and sincere in the request, chances are very good you would say, yes.

Job shadowing is a great way to get a glimpse of what the job entails and the atmosphere you would be working in. After doing a job shadow many students realize the job is a lot different than they thought and are able to prevent themselves from diving into a career they would not enjoy. Like informational interviews, a sincere interest in learning about the job is always your best approach.

Internships and Co-ops

Because they only last for a few months at most, internships and co-ops are low risk, full-out practice runs. Informational interviews, job shadowing, personal connections and your career center are the best way to get hooked up with internships and co-ops. A statistic we are going to repeat until you are sick of hearing it is that 64 percent of internships and co-ops lead to full-time employment. Before you graduate do as many as you can—shoot for at least three or four!

Take the first step in faith. You don't have to see the whole staircase. Just take the first step.

—Martin Luther King, Jr.

Words of Wisdom from LES:
I like observing and interviewing highly successful people.
I have had the opportunity to "analyze" over 200 suc-
cessful people, often for days at a time.

What struck me was the one common thread that united
all of these incredible people. Their work energizes them.
In other words, they display a genuine passion for what
they do. And it affects the people around them, business
colleagues, employees, even their family and friends.
What you've learned in this focusing strategy is a sure-fire
way to discover and ignite your fire within. This is priceless
information. Make sure you use it to your greatest advantage. One of the tragic things I observe on my travels is
the masses of people who are living without passion—wandering generalities just putting in time, just getting by.
There's no spark, no excitement—how sad. Be different!
Focus on discovering what will give you passion, or you'll
likely experience the devastating pain of regret later.
Who wants to be known as a wandering generality?

As you go through college you will uncover more and more
pieces of your Passion Puzzle™. The more pieces you discover,
the more synergies, obvious ties and career options you will see
before you. Continue to investigate the relationships among
the four components of your puzzle so you can have absolute
certainty that your career will give you passion. If passion is so
critical—and it obviously is—then what are you willing to do to
discover it? Will you take classes out of interest, rather than
just going for a high grade? Will you arrange informational
interviews, job shadowing, and internships and co-ops? Will
you make a commitment to complete your Passion Puzzle™?

CONCLUSION

Those individuals who are fueled with passion achieve higher levels of happiness and success.

Three Critical Concepts to Grasp the Power of Passion

1. Passion is an emotion that is created; it isn't one specific thing you discover.
2. Be passionate about the cause (your day-to-day work), not just the effect it creates (benefits, money, status).
3. It has been proven time and time again that when you have passion for your work, profits will follow.

Your Passion Puzzle™

- You will have passion for your work if: it aligns with what you value; allows you to express your interests; makes use of your skills and supports your ambitions.
- Your VISA is your passport to passion.

Harnessing the Power of the Puzzle

- Filling in your puzzle is an ongoing activity that is accelerated by taking part in new experiences.
- Search for jobs and careers that are in line with your puzzle.
- Share your puzzle with friends, career counselors and creative people who can help see synergies you might miss.

Investigate Your Career Ideas

- Informational interviews—find someone working in a job that you could be passionate about, set up an interview (lunch or a coffee), and pick his or her brains for advice.
- Job shadowing—for a day, shadow someone who works in a career you want to learn more about.
- Internships and co-ops—get out and give these a practice run while it's still risk free!

You can have a burning passion for many different careers, as long as they utilize your values, interests, skills and ambitions. What careers will give you passion? Find out by using *The Passion Check* in the following Action Steps.

Write your top values and skills in the puzzle—one in each puzzle piece

VALUES

VALUES

SKILLS

SKILLS

INTERESTS

INTERESTS

AMBITIONS

AMBITIONS

Write your top interests and ambitions in the puzzle—one in each puzzle piece

ACTION STEPS

Online version available in *The Focus Zone* at:
www.focusedstudent.com

Your Career Discovery List

Adding to Your Passion Puzzle™

The Passion Check

Online Assessments

Your Career Discovery List

Use the space below to write down career ideas and ideal job descriptions that utilize pieces from all four sections of your puzzle.

_____

_____

_____

_____

_____

_____

_____

_____

_____

Adding to Your Passion Puzzle™

Pick the job description or career idea from Your Career Discovery List that interests you the most and write it on the line below. (If you didn't write anything down in Your Career Discovery List, write below a career you think will give you passion):

_____

Choose three activities you can participate in that will help clarify if this career or job description is a good fit for you. (Examples: informational interviews, job shadowing, internships and co-ops, attending a conference or trade show, reading a book, etc.)

1. _____

_____

2. _____

_____

3. _____

_____

Remember this! After you participate in these activities, add any new insights you gained to your Passion Puzzle™.

The Passion Check

At the top of the table on the following page write the career idea or job description that you selected for the previous Action Step. In the center column, fill in the values, interests, skills and ambitions of an ideal candidate. In the last column place a check mark if *your* characteristics match at least 50 percent of them.

*CAREER: _____		
Passion Fuel	**Ideal Career Candidate**	**Do You Have It?**
VALUES		
INTERESTS		
SKILLS		
AMBITIONS		

How many check marks do you have? Shoot for a career that produces all four check marks, and your fire within will be ignited. *Use the search function at www.bls.gov/search/ooh.asp?ct=OOH if you want more information on the career you listed above.

FREE Online Assessments

Go to *The Focus Zone* at *www.focusedstudent.com* and check out the online Action Steps for Focusing Strategy #2. Included is a list of free career assessments that are fun, quick and easy. They will dramatically improve your clarity about what careers suit you best. If you are not sure you are taking the right major, these assessments are a must.

In the next focusing strategy you'll discover the four styles of work where your passion can be applied. Which style will be best for you? Let's find out.

Are You Headed in the Right Direction?

If the ladder is not leaning against the right wall, every step we take just gets us to the wrong place faster.

—Stephen Covey

The Passion Puzzle™ holds the key to igniting your passion. The next step in designing your ultimate career is to determine which style of work is best for you. We call this your career direction. You can channel what gives you passion in one of four directions. None of these four directions is any better than the other three, but we are all better suited to one direction over the others.

The challenge is to determine which direction best suits your values, interests, skills and ambitions so you can start climbing the right mountain, the one that provides the greatest joy and fulfillment throughout your life. Obviously, the direction you choose is critically important. Imagine huffing and puffing for years, as so many people do, climbing up this big mountain of a career, only to discover that the rewards of all that effort are minimal. Soon you're bored, hating the view and unhappy with the money you're earning. Is that what you want? We hope not. To avoid this painful scenario you need a compass.

Are you familiar with the standard compass? It will show you North, South, East and West. Well, toss it out! That compass may help you during a walk in the park, but it's not going to help you determine what career to pursue. You need a much more powerful direction finder called The Career Compass.

The Career COMPASS

E – Employee

S-B – Self-Employed/ Business Owner

P – Professional

A – Artist

As you learn more about the four major directions you will notice that they may or may not relate to your Passion Puzzle™. The more pieces of your Passion Puzzle™ you have filled in, the easier it will be to choose a direction. Later, we'll show you a few examples of people executing passion in various directions.

When it comes to choosing the best direction, you can do one of four things:

1. Live by the seat of your pants
Many people simply coast through life, living by the seat of their pants and taking little or no time to plan their future. People who say, "I dunno . . ." or "I'll just see what happens . . ." are coasters who go with the flow and allow their direction to choose them. The needle on their compass just keeps spinning wildly. At best, they have a one-in-four chance of coasting into the right direction.

"What career direction is best for you?"

2. Assume your family and friends know what is best

Have you ever watched a movie that you didn't like, one you found boring or downright awful? Did someone recommend this movie to you, perhaps a family member or friend? After a week of convincing and hype that it's the greatest movie since *Lord of the Rings,* you go see it, only to struggle through to the end, feeling like your miniscule $5 bag of popcorn was a better value. For some people, when it comes to choosing a career the same scenario often holds true. Your family and friends will recommend you do things *they* enjoy because it's made them successful. Your aunt the pharmacist might swear up and down that the pharmaceuticals field is best for you, while your dad gives you a sales pitch on the benefits of entrepreneurship.

They do so because they care about you and want to help. However, what they often overlook is that your values, interests, skills and ambitions are different. Beware! Choosing your future direction based on the opinions of your family and friends can end up like a very bad movie.

> Words of Wisdom from LES:
> Upon leaving high school, my parents advised me to find a good, secure job. Attending college wasn't on their radar screen. On reflection, I realize that this was the direction many people opted for back then—it was all they knew. Respecting my parents wishes, I spent 14 years going in the wrong direction. I worked as a hematology technologist in a large hospital. My hidden talent was to be an entrepreneur, and I also loved to write. Thankfully a wonderful mentor, Jim Rohn, helped me unlock these abilities and I now have the privilege of doing what I love—creating new products, writing, coaching and speaking. The message? Don't sabotage your future. Discover your real talent, then search for an environment that allows you to maximize your brilliance.

© The Power of Focus, 2005. CASEY JOHNSON

"Even though he was adopted, Joey's dad believed he was a Hayashi at heart."

3. Put college in control

Colleges share some responsibility when it comes to aligning students in a direction that may not be in their best interests. Remember, the school system was designed to educate people in specific disciplines. It wasn't designed to help people determine what gives them passion or what work style is best for them. Once enrolled in a faculty or field of study, it can seem quite challenging to change majors, let alone change faculties. For example, if you decide for whatever reason to enroll in the engineering program, that program will continue to train you to become an engineer. That's just the way it is. If you decide after your freshman or sophomore year that you're heading in the wrong direction, then it's up to you to change course. Generally speaking, colleges influence students to head in the employee or professional direction. A very important question to ask is: are you letting your program or major choose your direction?

4. Choose your own direction

The last, and best, option is to choose your own direction based on your values, interests, skills and ambitions—the things that stir up passion. It sounds so practical, doesn't it? However, few students realize this. Most go with the flow, allowing family and friends to guide them, or they simply accept the direction of their college program. By not choosing the direction that is best for you, grave consequences may show up later. Imagine the struggle of a highly paid dentist deciding to switch careers five years into his profession. Inevitably, a large pay cut would be part of the cost of this decision. Continuing mortgage payments along with the expense of raising a family might create all sorts of new pressures. Or how about the burned-out entrepreneur who now wishes she had chosen to work for a large corporation after graduating from college. She will likely end up selling the business or going into receivership. Either way she will be forced to start all over again. When she eventually finds a job, she will likely start near the bottom of the food chain, putting her years behind her friends and peers. As time goes by, making a transition from one direction to another becomes much more difficult. Choosing the best direction now, while you are still in school, will ensure your college degree is put to good use rather than causing a multitude of headaches and challenges in the future.

> There is no best direction, but one
> direction is best for you.

The first step is to recognize that you have a choice and that there are four directions to choose from. The next step is to compare the four work styles and choose the one that suits you best. The four directions to choose from are described below, with accompanying stories, examples and questions that will stimulate your mind and increase your clarity. Not only will you learn the ins and outs of each direction, you will also learn how to customize your college experience in a way that will maximize your future success. This is big stuff, so stay focused!

The Employee
DIRECTION

DEFINITION: Employees are employed by an organization or by individuals.

An employee is anyone from the vice president of a *Fortune* 500 company to a pizza delivery boy.

Did you know that four out of five students will become employees after graduation? This direction covers a wide range of jobs and is also known as the default direction, because this is where you will likely end up if you don't take time to consider the other three options. If you are excited by the line, "A safe and secure job with benefits and a steady paycheck," then this direction will interest you.

There are two big drawbacks to being an employee. The first is lack of control. As an employee you typically have a set amount of holidays and vacation time and are bound by a daily work schedule. Are you someone who values a lot of flexibility and control? If so, this direction may be frustrating at times—for example, if you want to take off early on a Friday to play a round of golf or prefer to work irregular hours.

The second drawback is that being an employee can limit your ability to become wealthy. Is becoming wealthy one of your ambitions? The reason it's difficult to become wealthy as an employee is because your earnings are directly linked to your time. An hour of work is traded for an hour of pay. Your schmoozing ability and skills might get you a raise or two, but those raises come in small increments and will very rarely make you a millionaire.

People who are the happiest employees are those who enjoy their work along with the security and comfort of a job that has good benefits and a predictable paycheck. Are your preferences and natural abilities more in line with the employee direction? If so, the following three things can help kick-start a successful journey as an employee.

THREE WAYS TO CUSTOMIZE YOUR COLLEGE EXPERIENCE FOR SUCCESS IN THE EMPLOYEE DIRECTION:

1. Differentiate

Hundreds of thousands of students graduate each year with the same degree. That's a lot of competition! To differentiate yourself from the pack, join clubs, volunteer, take on leadership roles and build your experience in areas that other students don't. What will make your resume stand out? What will make employers want to hire you?

2. Get to know the right people

Companies have huge budgets to recruit good employees. They send recruiters to events where they think good potential employees hang out. Events like student conferences, career fairs and competitions are common shopping grounds. If you don't stand out or, worse still, if you aren't even on the shelf, you won't get picked. If you are too impatient for the recruiters to come to you, go to them. Set up an information interview with a company you like or ask to job shadow one of their employees for the afternoon.

3. Participate in internships and co-ops

Numbers don't lie: 64 percent of interns are offered a job at their host company. If you want to become an employee, internships and co-ops will put the odds for immediate employment in your favor.

The S-B
DIRECTION

Ben Barry is a cool young guy from Ottawa, Canada.
At 22 he's the owner of a fast-growing modeling agency that chooses to reflect society more accurately by showcasing models of all ages, sizes, races and abilities. Currently he has 250 people on his roster. He is also graduating from university this year with a double major in business and woman's studies—a very appropriate combination considering the nature of his work. And get this. At 18 Ben was on *Oprah,* after being spotted by one of her producers when he won a *Teen People* magazine award. After the show his office was flooded with 500,000 emails, all of which he replied to . . . but that's another story.

So how did Ben decide that entrepreneurship was his calling? When he was 14, one of his friends decided she wanted to be a model, so after investing $3,000 in a course she began approaching agencies. They all turned her down. She was absolutely gutted. Young Ben thought his friend was talented and beautiful, so he sent some photos to a local studio on her behalf. Lo and behold, a few weeks later they called him back saying they wanted to book her. The person on the phone asked, "Are you her agent?" Was he supposed to lie? Of course he was her agent, or at least he was after the phone call. He was only in eighth grade. Other friends followed suit, and since eighth grade the Ben Barry Agency has added clients like Sears, Nike, Dove and MTV.

With his business so successful, why would Ben bother going to college? He says: "It's important to take advantage of the unique experience that college provides. It's a small window of time compared to your whole life. I've spoken to many entrepreneurs who totally regret missing out on the college experience. The bottom line is you can do both, own a business and have a great education."

At age 14 Ben became self-employed. He was ambitious, persistent and wanted to make a difference in the world. Ben didn't let the uncertainty of starting a business bother him— he stayed dedicated to his cause and was willing to take the necessary risks. The rewards were tremendous and are a great example of the difference one can make and the success one can have by choosing the S-B direction.

If you choose this direction you'll find highs and lows as well as big risks and big returns. Your income may be sporadic and will depend on your skill set, persistence and street smarts combined with your book smarts. The biggest distinguishing factor about this direction is that you work for yourself and have full control of what you do, how much you earn, and when and where you work. You have all the fun, and you also bear all the risk.

Answer these questions to determine if this direction is a good fit for you:

- Do I like being in control, even if it means working on weekends?

- Can I tolerate high levels of risk? (four out of five businesses fail within the first few years)

- Am I willing to fail more than once before I hit it big?

- Am I adventurous? Or am I the one that orders chicken fingers and fries at every dinner outing?

- Am I willing to be an entrePOORneur before I am a successful entrepreneur?

- Does my Passion Puzzle™ have words like predictability, routine, stability and security in it? If so, entrepreneurship may not be for me.

- Does my Passion Puzzle™ have "start my own business" in the ambitions or interests section?

- Did I show entrepreneurial spirit when I was young (lemonade stands included)? Is entrepreneurship in my blood?

"S" is for
SELF-EMPLOYED

DEFINITION: Self-employed people, as the name makes blatantly obvious, work for themselves and not for someone else, or someone else's company.

Self-employed individuals can be very similar to employees in that their earnings rely on their presence and participation. A Mom and Pop convenience store is a typical example. If you don't show up to work you don't get paid.

Superman and Superwoman
were self-employed.

When Ben Barry started his modeling agency, he only made money when he found work for his clients. If Ben didn't make the phone calls, there was no cash coming in. As Ben grew his business, he increased his earnings by hiring employees. Ben's salary was no longer limited to how many phone calls he could make in a day; he had other people making these phone calls for him. To make the transition from being self-employed to being a business owner you must gradually build a great team and create efficient systems. This allows the business to operate without you being present 24/7.

"B" is for
BUSINESS OWNER

DEFINITION: A business owner is someone who owns a business that operates smoothly without his or her total involvement.

Think Donald Trump, one of America's greatest real estate developers and multibillionaire. His rapidly growing empire includes award-winning restaurants, luxury apartments, casinos, golf courses and recently Trump University (check it out). He also contributes significant time and money to various charitable organizations. With more than 20,000 employees, Donald Trump uses leverage to create a smooth-running business conglomerate. He hires great people to run his various projects. This frees him up to dream about the next big thing or to play golf every week, which he also enjoys. "The Donald" has mastered the art of becoming a business owner.

Being a business owner is like being a car manufacturer. You need to build the car in such a way that other people can drive it. Imagine designing a car that only one person can drive! To become a successful business owner you first need to build a profitable business that others can drive, so you can focus solely on the few things you do best.

Unless you have piles of money to buy an existing business, becoming a business owner will take time. You will likely need to turn on the jet engines to get the business off the ground and then start building systems and a good team so that it runs smoothly without you being involved in every little detail.

Yes, this takes work, but the potential payoffs are very attractive. Business owners can earn a lot more money by leveraging their time through other people and creating efficient systems. This gives you more freedom to sit on a beach if you wish, or to use the extra time to make the world a better place. You don't need to become the next Donald Trump to be a business owner, but if you do want to become a billionaire this is your only option.

THREE WAYS TO CUSTOMIZE YOUR COLLEGE EXPERIENCE FOR SUCCESS IN THE S-B DIRECTION:

1. Attend business plan competitions
There are many of these around the country that you can participate in. Why wait until you are in the real world to see if your brilliant business idea will pan out? These competitions will allow you to organize your ideas and have them critiqued by esteemed judges. Also, it's not uncommon to find an investor in attendance who may offer you serious money to help get your idea into motion.

2. Get mentored
Being a student gives you a full deck of "I'm a student" cards to play. Successful entrepreneurs get great satisfaction from helping eager students (such as yourself). Pick someone you admire and ask for an hour of time once a month. Use that time to pick his or her brain and get advice. You'll be surprised how much a mentor will enjoy coaching you and to what lengths they will go to help you succeed.

3. Flex your entrepreneurial muscle
College, for the most part, will teach you theory. To be a successful entrepreneur you will need to learn how to put this theory into practice. Get involved in the programs, courses and extracurricular activities that will give you the hands-on training you need. Check out organizations

like www.SIFE.org and www.C-E-O.org that offer unique experiences for aspiring entrepreneurs. Also, join an entrepreneurship club on campus and hang out with the like-minded students. The more entrepreneurs you associate with, the more ideas you'll come up with and the more they will be supported. To take your entrepreneurship training to the next level, look into courses offered by Trump University. They focus on learning by doing, which is critical for entrepreneurs.

Your summer breaks are also valuable training grounds. Rather than being in a stuffy office working for a large company, test a business idea, work alongside an entrepreneur. This will give you invaluable business experience. In addition, if you want to learn from the best business leaders in the world, simply buy their books. Colleges can't afford to hire these big ballers to teach you one on one, but for as little as $10 you can learn all their secrets. Check out the resource guide at the back of this book for some recommended titles.

The Professional
DIRECTION

DEFINITION: A professional is someone with very specialized knowledge, usually gained after long and intensive academic preparation.

Typical examples include dentist, lawyer, architect, pharmacist, professor, doctor and optometrist.

If you are having a hard time determining if an occupation is a profession, give the Parent Test a whirl.

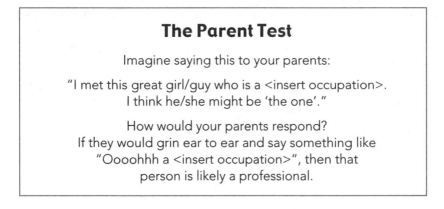

The Parent Test

Imagine saying this to your parents:

"I met this great girl/guy who is a <insert occupation>.
I think he/she might be 'the one'."

How would your parents respond?
If they would grin ear to ear and say something like
"Oooohhh a <insert occupation>", then that
person is likely a professional.

Professionals get a lot of respect and admiration from society, including our parents. Why not? They deserve this high level of respect because they provide a valuable service to society. Do you like the sound of this?

If your Passion Puzzle contains words like status, prestige, respect or responsibility (or something similar), the professional direction may be just your ticket. Another thing: professionals are always in demand. You don't see many doctors and dentists in unemployment lines. Professionals have high levels of job security, which is great for those who value security and tend to be risk-averse.

Does that sound like you? Analytical skills, attention to detail, good reasoning and problem-solving ability are some common skills required by professionals. Good professionals can perform under pressure, solve an array of problems and enjoy learning. Does that describe you?

Questionable reasons for becoming a professional:

- **Why not?** Do you know anyone who fits the following description? They finish their undergraduate degree but still have no idea what they want to do. Because they aren't ready to face the real world and they have decent grades, they decide to go to law school, do their masters or pursue their PhD. If you don't have a friend that fits this description, you might have a few professors that do—these are typically the bad ones. Fear of entering the real world is not a good reason to spend a few more years in school (and a lot more money) pursuing a profession you may have no aptitude for.

- **Big bucks.** Professionals have high incomes. Contrary to popular belief, however, this is not the direction you get rich in, because your earnings are tied to your time. Professionals get paid for how many clients they see, how many surgeries they perform or how many cases they work on. If they don't work, they don't get paid. Are you pursuing a profession because of the money?

> Caution: Becoming a professional
> is a big investment.

The road is long. It starts with an undergrad degree accompanied by high grades. Then comes more school and specialized training, or plenty of work experience. Most professions require that you are in school for at least six years and many require closer to 10 years. This is a lot of time focused on preparing for a single profession, not to mention the enormous student loans that can come with it. On top of the time and money, you are extremely specialized as a professional. If a brain surgeon decides he or she is bored doing surgery on brains, it will be difficult to switch career directions while maintaining a similar lifestyle. If you are always changing your mind, if you don't like to stay with one thing for a long time, then this might not be a good choice for you. If you are thinking of becoming a professional, can you visualize yourself working in this profession 10, 20 or 30 years from now?

THREE WAYS TO CUSTOMIZE YOUR COLLEGE EXPERIENCE FOR SUCCESS IN THE PROFESSIONAL DIRECTION:

1. Focus on high grades

You will need high grades to get into law school or medical school or any other specialized professional program. The better your grades, the better chance you have of getting into the grad school of your choice.

2. Double check

Do an internship or become a research assistant working with a professional who does what you want to do. It is important to ensure you love the profession you are going into. The best way to confirm your decision is to get some hands-on experience.

3. Act like a professional

Every profession has an association, trade show, conference or annual convention—get involved! Act as if you are already a dentist or an architect by attending events and reading publications related to your profession. You will make great contacts who can help you in securing a job long before you graduate.

The Artist
DIRECTION

DEFINITION: An artist is someone who uses imagination, talent or skill to create works of aesthetic value. Examples include singers, songwriters, illustrators, sculptors, novelists, dancers, comedians and actors/actresses.

Professional athletes also fall under this definition because great athletes have honed their skills to an art form.

What do Michael Jordan, Madonna and Michelangelo all have in common? Okay, they all start with the letter M, but what else? The answer is that they all do or did something extremely well. This is the basis of the artist direction. Those who are successful as artists don't necessarily need to be a Michelangelo, but they need to have a talent for something. Do you have a talent or a skill that is truly outstanding? Perhaps you can act, play the piano or throw a football? Do you have a superb skill that is undeniable in your Passion Puzzle™? If so, then the artist direction could be very lucrative for you. However, in addition to talent, a few other ingredients are needed to sculpt a successful career as an artist.

"I was born with music inside me."

This simple statement by a young kid called Ray speaks volumes. Born in 1930, during the Depression years, poverty was thrust upon Ray and his family. At the age of six he began losing his sight due to glaucoma. One of his last sights was witnessing his brother drown in the washtub his mother used to clean the laundry. He spent eight years at the St. Augustine School for the Deaf and Blind where he learned piano, clarinet and alto saxophone, as well as writing music in Braille. At 15 he was orphaned, losing his greatest source of inspiration, his mother.

Young Ray had two things going for him that made a huge difference: first he was determined to overcome all the challenges that life would throw at him. Second, he believed in himself and his passion—the world of music. Knowing he was gifted, he made a commitment to bring his evolving talent to the marketplace. It was tough slogging at first—at times he almost starved and he was often short-changed because he was blind. The owner of a small record company, Swingtime Records, recognized his talent and gave him his first record deal. The days of performing solo for peanuts in small piano bars were over. He formed a band and started making records. That was when the genius of Ray Charles was born. Hit records such as "Georgia on my Mind" confirmed his celebrity. For more than 50 years the incredible talent of Ray Charles blessed people around the world. His unique style transcended every musical genre from rhythm and blues, to gospel, to rock 'n' roll to country. His awards and accomplishments are too numerous to mention here. The bottom line? Ray knew he was a great artist and he gave his gift to the world.

The story of Ray Charles highlights the essential ingredients (in addition to extraordinary talent) that an artist needs to achieve success:

1. Believe in yourself.
2. Overcome challenges.
3. Bring your talent to the market.

Although it can be a struggle to get your talent recognized, and during that time cash and security are often hard to find, success in the artist direction can be huge. Ray Charles was willing to tackle any obstacle thrown his way and, with the help of Swingtime Records, he found a way to bring his talent to the market. Do you believe in your talent? Are you willing to overcome obstacles? Will you work diligently to find someone with the experience and contacts needed to bring your talent to the market? If you answered yes to these three questions, like Ray Charles, you can do it too.

"Mom, I have something to tell you . . . I want to start a rock band!"

What will Mom say?

She might say something like, "You have a better chance of being hit by lightning!"

Heading in this direction is often uncomfortable for parents because they are concerned you might fail. Be prepared for resistance. Follow your heart and do what is best for you—it's your life to live.

If you think of five famous people, the odds are that at least four of them are artists. Do you have fame and fortune in your Passion Puzzle™? Are you willing to do what it takes to achieve it? Something unique about the artist direction is that you get to indulge in honing your individuality and creativity. Does being liberated and creative sound appealing to you?

THREE WAYS TO CUSTOMIZE YOUR COLLEGE EXPERIENCE FOR SUCCESS IN THE ARTIST DIRECTION:

1. Contacts, contacts, contacts

Do you think you are the only one who wants to move to Hollywood to star in the next blockbuster? The person who gets the chance will be the person who knows the director, the producer, the assistant producer or the water boy. College gives you access to a wide variety of events and opportunities where great contacts can be made. Art exhibits, dance performances, independent films, TV commercials, castings, baseball games and book fairs are a few examples. Don't rely on your college to inform you of these opportunities or to bring these great events to you. The possibilities are endless in any given city. Look for the ones related to your talent, get involved and connect with the people there. The more contacts you have in your chosen indus-try, and the more experience you have working in it, the better your odds are of making it big.

2. Practice, practice, practice

If you are good at something, practice and hone that skill so you become brilliant at it. Remember, talent is a key ingredient to being a successful artist. College is an incredible training ground for artists just by the sheer number of courses offered and clubs around. Don't let these opportunities slip away—make practicing your talent a part of your daily college routine. As a teenager, Jim Carrey spent hours in front of his bathroom mirror making crazy faces and doing comical impersonations. He now earns $20 million per movie.

3. Build a team of experts

So you're a great swimmer and you want to go to the Olympics. Find someone who also thinks you are a great swimmer and can help make you into an Olympian. While you are in college, coaches are often FREE—take advantage of these offerings while you can! In addition to a coach, look for someone who has business or marketing savvy that can sell you and your talent to the world. Most struggling artists try to do it all themselves but lack marketing ability or don't have any interest in this important aspect of the business. Use your college events, resource centers and programs to help find someone who has the ability to bring your talent to the market.

Have you decided which direction is best for you? Do you want to be an employee with a steady paycheck? Do you want to take on the high risk and high return of starting your own business? Do you want the admiration and respect of being a professional? Or do you want to hone a talent and become an artist? Remember, there is no one-fits-all best direction, but there is a best direction for you.

Passion + Direction = ULTIMATE CAREER

Imagine a career where you show up at work early and stay late because you're having so much fun. An environment where you enjoy the people, are interested in the day-to-day tasks and are constantly moving toward your goals. A job you don't view as work, but as recreation you get paid for. Do you think such a reality exists? For most people this is only a fantasy, but it's possible for anyone to live this reality. It's what we call your ultimate career, a career that's in line with your values, interests, skills and ambitions and is in the direction that suits you best.

Right now you might feel overwhelmed and uncertain as to what this is. Don't fret, worry, cry or throw this book out the window. For most people, this is normal. By continuing to fill in your Passion Puzzle™ the picture of your ultimate career will eventually start to shine through—perhaps it already has. Choosing a direction is your single best way to shortlist your options and make the search much less daunting. Best of all, choosing a direction will allow you to customize your college experience so you make the most of it. And that's no cliché statement—this stuff really works!

The Action Steps that follow will help you take the next big step in uncovering your ultimate career. In the next few chapters you'll start developing the skills essential for success that aren't taught in the classroom. Stay tuned.

CONCLUSION

The direction you choose is critically important. Making the right choice now will save you a lot of time, energy and money, later.

The Career COMPASS

The Employee Direction

- More stability and security, but less control and your income is linked to your time. Four out of five graduates will become employees. CUSTOMIZE COLLEGE FOR SUCCESS:

Differentiate yourself, get to know the right people and participate in internships and co-ops.

The S-B Direction

- Self-employed people are those who run their own business. When you are no longer needed in the day-to-day operations of your business you become a business owner. Are you willing to take on the high risk and uncertainty of starting your own business? Although the hours are long, business owners can make big bucks because their income is not tied to their time.

CUSTOMIZE COLLEGE FOR SUCCESS:

Attend business plan competitions, get mentored and gain practical business experience.

The Professional Direction

- Requires lots of school but leads to job security and admiration from others. Is the most challenging direction to switch out of later in life.

CUSTOMIZE COLLEGE FOR SUCCESS:

Focus on high grades, attend events related to your profession and double-check if the profession is right for you.

The Artistic Direction

- Do you have impressive talent in an art or a sport? If so, you're halfway there. You need to believe in yourself, be

ready to overcome challenges, and take your talent to market in order to excel in this direction.
CUSTOMIZE COLLEGE FOR SUCCESS:
Make contacts in the industry, practice like crazy and build a team of experts and coaches.

Your Ultimate Career

- A career that is in line with your values, interests, skills and ambitions and is in the direction that is best for you.

Take time to clearly study your options. There is a best direction for you. The following Action Steps will give you a clearer picture.

ACTION STEPS

Online version available in *The Focus Zone* at:
www.focusedstudent.com

Choose Your Direction

Your Ultimate Career

Choose Your Direction

Which direction interests you the most? If you are having a tough time deciding between two directions, write down the one you would pursue if you could only choose one and money didn't matter.

_____

Flip back to the three ways to customize your college experience for success in this direction (E – p. 76, S-B – p. 81, P – p. 85, A – p. 88). Choose one of these strategies and describe how and when you will implement it below:

_____

_____

_____

Your Ultimate Career (the most important Action Step)

Refer to Your Career Discovery List on page 66. How do the ideal job descriptions and career ideas you wrote down relate to the direction you have chosen? If you wrote a specific career—deep sea photographer, social worker, etc.—then double-check to make sure the direction this career relates to is the direction that is best for you. Remember, for it to be an ultimate career it must combine values, interests, skills and ambitions *and* be in the direction that you prefer.

If you wrote a job description like *working in fashion—doing writing and teaching—flexible hours—recognition and prestige—potential to write a book,* then, to determine an ultimate career option, combine your ideal job description with your preferred direction. Using this example, a person who chose the Employee direction might define an ultimate career as "editor of a well-known fashion magazine," while someone who chose the S-B direction might define it to be "own and operate a fashion publi-cation business" and someone choosing the Artist direction might say "freelance writer for a well-known fashion magazine." So, look at Your Career Discovery List and at your selected direction and write two ideas below that could be ultimate careers for you.

1. _____

2. _____

Your Habits
Determine Your Future

We are what we repeatedly do.
Excellence then, is not an
act, but a habit.

—Aristotle

Jack Burton loved selling.
As a five-year-old kid he had the most successful lemonade stand on the block. Next, it was going door-to-door selling Christmas cards. Then in his early teens he developed the biggest paper route in the neighborhood. At age 15 Jack helped his dad run his roofing company, turning estimates into sales. At college he had fun, but he also made money on weekends working for a local painting company, where he turned quotes into contracts. Now with a marketing degree adding another level of credibility to his resume, Jack was ready to take on the world. He was interviewed by an international training organization for a position selling change management workshops to large corporations, an opportunity he was really excited about. At 23, Jack was perfect for the job. Not only was he immaculately dressed and well prepared, he had solid presentation skills, an impressive track record and a competitive nature. The interview went well.

Back in the boardroom, after Jack had left, the senior corporate officers weighed their decision. They all agreed that Jack had the right attitude, sales ability, appropriate education and experience. However, there was one thing they couldn't overlook. The final decision was unanimous. Jack would not be hired due to one bad habit—personal hygiene. To put it bluntly, he had really, really bad breath.

In case you're wondering if we made this story up, we didn't. Unfortunately, it's true. To protect his identity we've changed the young man's name.

This chapter is all about habits. Your habits will determine how your future works out—good or bad. And as you've just realized through Jack's experience, sometimes it's the little things that can trip you up and ruin a great opportunity. In this fast-paced Information Age you are hired for who you are and for what you bring to the company. Instead of just one specific skill set, or your degree qualifications, your opportunities are based on everything you bring to the table, including your habits! College can be a breeding ground for creating great habits, ones that will set you up for a lifetime of success and prosperity. Alternatively, the college environment can also spawn an outbreak of bad habits and significantly limit your future opportunities. What habits will you acquire?

> *The second half of a man's life is made up*
> *of nothing but the habits he has*
> *acquired during the first half.*
>
> —Feodor Dostoevski

Have you chosen to adopt the experience-focused mindset you learned about in Focusing Strategy #1? We hope so. The first component of this mindset involved implementing the experience-focused formula (exchange programs + internships and co-ops + extracurricular activities + innovative programs).

The second stage involved designing your ultimate career by piecing together your Passion Puzzle™ and discovering the career direction that is best for you.

The next stage of the experience-focused mindset involves developing successful habits—the part our mouthwash-lacking friend Jack was missing. Habits are the practical day-to-day disciplines; the glue that holds everything together as you march forward toward your ultimate career. In this focusing strategy we'll show you a powerful three-step formula for transforming any bad habit into a successful one. In addition, we'll share six top study habits of successful students —stuff that 4.0 students at Ivy League schools do. These simple habits will relieve you of a lot of unneeded stress and save you a ton of time so you can focus more on the amazing experiences that college offers.

"After being transferred from the floral department to the paint department, Jenny's compulsive smelling habit began affecting her performance."

What is
A HABIT

Simply stated, a habit is something you do so often that it becomes easy and automatic. You might get in the habit of being five minutes late for class or going to the gym at 8 A.M. every morning. The cool thing is you can program yourself to adopt any habit you like. This will allow you to replace the bad habits with good ones so you can expand your potential rather than limit it.

Understand this. You are your habits—they are responsible for up to 90 percent of your behavior. Habits guide your actions and reactions and are the reflection people see of you. Can you think of a few bad habits that reflect an image you dislike? Not to worry, we'll get rid of those bad ones a little later.

> Successful people have successful habits
> —unsuccessful people don't.

The payoff for developing successful habits is HUGE! Consider this: wealthy people have wealthy habits—ask them. Healthy people have healthy habits—observe them. Weird people have weird habits—it's obvious. Happy people have figured out what makes them happy and they practice it daily. In other words, they make it a habit.

The habits you develop from this day forward will ultimately determine how your future works out—healthy or unhealthy, fulfilled or unfulfilled, happy or miserable, rich or poor, enjoying loving relationships or being alone.

Brand this knowledge into your consciousness forever—it's that important.

WARNING

The people you hang around with and
the environment you live in greatly
influence your habits.

Be careful to develop the habits *you* want.

Don't allow a negative environment or other people
to impose bad habits on you.

College is your personal training ground, and developing successful habits is an essential part of a good training routine. Creating successful habits takes time and discipline, but once a new habit is developed it becomes part of your normal behavior and will be harder to break than it is to keep.

Consequences arrive later

For every action you take, there are consequences. It sucks, but it's true. Depending on the habit, the consequences can be as sweet as a cupcake or as bad as a rotten apple. It is your continual negative behavior that claims the not-so-glamorous title—bad habits. And often, the consequences of your bad habits don't show up until much later in life. Some people (hopefully not you) find this out the hard way.

Barb Tarbox was one of these people.

Unusually tall for her age, in grade seven Barb felt like an outcast. She desperately wanted to be cool and accepted by her peers, but low self-esteem restricted her confidence. Despite her striking good looks she seemed destined to be a loner. One day she noticed that the "cool" kids all had something in common—they smoked. Barb realized this could be her ticket to new friends and, more importantly, to being accepted. It worked! At 11 years old, she started smoking.

Fast forward her story to 30 years later. With a successful modeling career behind her, Barb is happily married to Pat and mother to Mackenzie, her much-loved daughter. But her life is in crisis. She has just been diagnosed with stage-four lung cancer and the prognosis is grim, with little hope of survival. The cause is obvious—the habit of smoking has finally caught up with her. The consequences, although not evident to her at age 11, are deadly.

Determined not to die without leaving a message about her tobacco addiction, Barb embarked on a year-long nation-wide tour of junior and senior high schools. Her relentless speaking schedule attracted the media's attention. TV, radio, magazines and newspapers ran major stories about this lone crusader who was telling young people, "Don't end up like me—I'll be dead in a few months and I'm only 42 years old!"

Barb wore a leopard print hat when she spoke to school groups. She would yank it off to show her bald head. "This is what chemotherapy does," she'd say, tears rolling down her cheeks. "My bones stick out of every area of my body now. My feet and my legs are blue, all because of smoking. Those of you that smoke, is this what you want?" Her talk often left children and parents in tears. Two months before she died, Barb reached her goal of bringing her message to more than 50,000 teens. Just before she passed away, her six-foot frame weighed a haunting 85 pounds.

The point we want to reinforce here is this:

> The results of your bad habits often don't
> show up in your life until much later.

This is a big deal, and the sooner you grasp this the more likely you are to minimize the chance of future disasters. Bad habits today can lead to poverty, loneliness, huge stress and sadly, like Barb, an early death.

Successful Habits
FOR STUDENTS

Do you know someone who always gets super high marks and seems to study far less than you do? Isn't it frustrating? If you want to be this student—getting high marks with minimal effort—pay close attention to the following six habits. These are the habits of top-performing students, and they are easy to adopt and make your own.

Habit #1—Always find the answers

The only thing rarer than good cafeteria food is the day a student doesn't have a single question. Whether it's needing clarity on exam topics, details for an assignment or clarification of a concept from a professor with a thick accent, students always have dozens of questions. The brightest students find answers to these questions; the struggling students don't.

Make it a habit: For each course, dedicate a few pages in your notebook or binder as "question pages". Anytime you have a question related to that course, immediately write it down in the question pages for that course. As your question pages grow—and before they turn into a novel—chase down the answers from your professor, a friend in class or a trusty textbook. It will only take a few weeks for this to become a habit. This will keep you on top of your game and drastically reduce your anxiety while studying for exams.

Habit #2—Review your notes

A study of Cornell University students revealed an interesting secret of the top performers. The students with a GPA of 3.7 or higher all had one thing in common—they reviewed their notes within five hours of taking them. How often do you review your notes?

It has been proven time and time again that we only retain 10 percent of what we read and only 50 percent of what we see and hear. However, if this information is reviewed within 24 hours, the retention rate soars to 80 percent. Obviously, students who retain 80 percent of what they learn are going to have a better GPA than students who only retain 10 to 50 percent.

Make it a habit: Whether it's after class, late afternoon, just before you go to sleep or exactly five hours later—review your notes the *same day* you take them.

LUC:
One of my classmates used to always carry a clipboard with blank paper—no backpack, no notebook, no binder —just a clipboard. I used to think he was crazy. I changed

my mind when I found out he had one of the highest GPAs in the class. When I quizzed him about his unusual habit, he explained that at the end of the day he would take his notes from his clipboard and put them into a series of binders labeled by subject. He did this so he couldn't help but review his notes at the end of each day. Obviously it worked.

Habit #3—Plan, don't cram

Do you currently write all exam dates, assignment deadlines, important appointments and homework into a day-planner of some kind? If so, you have already mastered this habit—congrats! If not, don't worry, this habit is easy to develop and will relieve you of tons of stress, not to mention free up valuable memory.

Make it a habit: The brain cannot be expected to remember all the homework assignments, meetings, exam dates and parties of your hectic student schedule. Delegate this burden to a day-planner, PDA (Palm Pilot, Pocket PC, BlackBerry, etc.), or the calendar on your cell phone. Making this a habit will greatly reduce the stress of uncertainty and prevent you from forgetting important due dates. When you plan, you can avoid having to cram.

Habit #4—Synergy

Have you ever been playing a team sport with a friend and—out of nowhere—magic seemed to happen? Together you were capable of making plays and scoring points that you never could have done by yourself. This phenomenon is called synergy. It occurs when two people work together and achieve far more than they could have on their own—where 1+1 = a lot more than 2. This can happen on the basketball court, the football field, the hockey rink and in school (no, we're not talking about cheating!). Finding someone in the same program or major who shares similar goals is a profound way to increase your success as a student. Creating a study-buddy relationship with this person will allow you to achieve much more than you could by yourself. By supporting and challenging each other to meet common goals, you'll gain incredible momentum and noteworthy results.

Find ways to make 1+1

equal more than 2.

Make it a habit: Do you have a perfect study buddy in mind? Perhaps you know someone, or maybe you need to start looking. Ask to work with this person on the next assignment or to study with him or her for your next exam. If the relationship is a good fit and you share similar academic goals, you both will experience a magical synergy and accomplish much more in less time. Make it a habit to continue working with this friend. You will soon have someone to rely on when you miss a class, don't understand an assignment or need help with a question. Best of all, you will have someone to test your knowledge before an exam.

Habit #5—Live by your customized study system

In college you must complete various tasks—writing papers, submitting assignments, preparing for exams etc. To be a successful student, you need to be successful at each task. An easy wayto achieve success is to have an efficient system for each task. Whether your system involves studying weeks before an exam or cramming the night before, or using flash cards insteadof multicolored notes, is completely up to you. What's more important is that you make the effort to develop a customized way of completing each task so you can produce the results you want. Do you like the idea of homework and studying becoming easier? When you find a system that yields the resultsyou want, stick to it and these once-painful tasks will become easier and easier.

Make it a habit: Do you have a customized method of writing papers, completing assignments and studying for exams? Is this method giving you the results you want? A little experimentation and you will soon discover a system that works best for you. Once you find the system that works best, make using it a habit. When an exam or assignment is approaching, all you will need to do is follow the system, step by step, and you'll get optimal results. It's that simple when you make it a habit.

Treasure #5—this is a freebee you won't want to miss. Go to *The Focus Zone* at *www.focusedstudent.com* to receive *"Mind Mastery–the top three memorization techniques used by the world's brightest students."* Out of these three memorization techniques, find the one that jives best with you and make it a part of your customized study system.

Habit #6—Insights & Ideas book
Did you know that Sir Richard Branson, the owner of Virgin Records, Virgin Airlines, Virgin Mobile, Virgin Books, Virgin Megastores and also, believe it or not, Virgin Student, carries a notepad around with him religiously every day to record his best ideas and insights?

Have you ever had a brilliant idea in the middle of the night? You wake up at four in the morning with this amazing concept, then you drift back to sleep and wake up hours later, only to find the idea has gone, like a puff of smoke, evaporated. Jim Rohn, one of the world's most respected business philosophers and a best-selling author, makes this comment: "Don't trust your memory. Develop the habit of immediately capturing every meaningful idea or insight that erupts in your brain." The key word is capture. If you don't grab those life-changing ideas right away, they often disappear seconds later because you are interrupted by a phone or you drift back to sleep.

Get in the habit of recording the things that are important to you, even if it's a good book, movie or a cool course someone recommended. Capture it!

Make it a habit: Create your own Insights & Ideas book— find a small notepad, open a memo or word-to-go document in your PDA, or reserve the last few pages in your day-planner. Whatever you decide to use, make it something that you carry with you all the time; you never know when your mind will churn out a brilliant idea or someone will recommend something you don't want to forget.

This includes good courses to take, events you just cannot miss, great books you should read, earth-shattering advice, needed inventions and business ideas. You'll be amazed at how many great insights and ideas you will capture over the course of a semester. Don't let another spark of wisdom be wasted— start your Insights & Ideas book now.

The Ultimate Habit: INTEGRITY

There is one habit that will always rank at the top of the importance list, whether you are a student, professional, entrepreneur or hippie. If you want to enjoy the flow of life rather than feeling like life is a constant struggle, the habit of integrity is a necessity. Simply put, integrity means doing what you say when you say you're going to do it—following through on your promises to completion.

Integrity is something you either have or you don't. It's black and white, cut and dried. Just as it's impossible to be a little bit pregnant (you are or you aren't), you can't dabble with integrity. People who have integrity go out of their way to maintain it. Those who don't wonder why relationships fall apart, opportunities don't come their way or money doesn't flow to them. Think of it like a light switch—your integrity switch is either on or off. Simply becoming aware of when you are acting with integrity (when it's on) and when you are acting out of integrity (when it's off) will put you far ahead of the pack. When you act with integrity, you will literally see the difference in how people treat you. Try it for a semester. We bet you'll never go back.

> *Honesty is conforming our words to*
> *our actions; integrity is conforming*
> *our actions to our words.*
>
> —Stephen Covey

People with integrity are trusted, respected and well liked. Living with integrity means acting in a way that builds trust, respect and admiration in all of your day-to-day interactions and relationships. We repeat—this all-important integrity factor must be ingrained in your day-to-day way of life, like wearing deodorant. Failing to act with integrity can ruin your relationships and seriously damage your reputation (like not wearing deodorant). In Focusing Strategy #7 we'll show you how all broken relationships can be traced back to broken agreements. In other words, all broken relationships can be traced back to a person who has not developed the habit of integrity.

FOUR SIMPLE WAYS TO DEVELOP INTEGRITY:

1. Don't make a promise you cannot keep

A lot of people have a hard time saying no—these people typically hate confrontation and will say yes to maintain a favorable impression. As a result, they make promises they cannot keep, and their integrity goes down the tubes.

ANDREW:
It was time to start planning our annual Super Bowl ski trip. It was one of the best parties of the year, with skiing, snowboarding, hot tubs and football—everything you

could possibly ask for. As the event drew near, however, our council became deeply concerned. The girl who was spear-heading the event planning was falling behind on her responsibilities. Prices weren't confirmed, rooms weren't booked and transportation was uncertain.

Every deadline and responsibility she promised to us was slipping through the cracks. She was rightfully busy with schoolwork and that was understandable, but what wasn't understandable was the way she dealt with the situation. At our weekly club meetings her updates were always positive—but they were candy-coated lies about how things were coming together nicely. Weeks went by with unfulfilled promises and the frustration among our team members soared. In the end, the event was a failure and the club suffered greatly from the negative impact. We had the lowest turnout in club history and lost hundreds of dollars. What the girl lost was much greater—respect. She wasn't aware that her integrity switch was turned off. Needless to say, she wasn't re-elected the following year.

The solution is simple: Don't make a promise you cannot keep. If someone asks you to do something, think about it and only say yes if you are absolutely, positively sure that you will be able to keep the promise. If not, say no. They will respect your honesty, your integrity will be maintained and your relationship will remain strong. If you are struggling to maintain a promise, your integrity (and reputation) will depend on how you handle the situation. If you put your ego aside and are open and honest about the challenges you are having, your integrity will be salvaged and so will your relationships.

2. Remember what you promise to others

Has a friend ever promised to call you, or return something, but they never did? How did you feel: frustrated, upset, angry? Did you lose a little faith or trust in the person because of it? You probably did. Now let's turn the tables around. How often are you the person who forgets to fulfill a promise? How do you think the person on the receiving end feels about your empty promise? These are usually the little things—promises you can keep, but simply forget about.

The solution is simple: If you promise someone something— an e-mail, phone call, money, etc.—be aware that you are putting your integrity on the line. Write it down IMMEDIATELY —in your schedule, on a napkin, on the back of your hand or staple a note to your butt if you want—anywhere to make sure you remember it. A good way to prevent memory overload and unnecessary stress is to avoid making too many promises. Put the ball in the other person's court. Say "Call me," rather than "I'll call you."

3. Always tell the truth

Do you know any chronic liars? Do you trust what these people say? There is something about lying that makes it so darned obvious. A stutter in the voice, a guilty glance, avoiding eye contact . . . whatever it may be, it never pays to lie. If you want people to trust you, then always tell the truth. When you face tough situations being honest might seem incredibly challenging. However, being up-front and honest in these situations will skyrocket the trust people have in you like nothing else.

4. Emphasize your integrity and make it a habit

When you send an e-mail with information, or an attachment you promised someone, start the e-mail with "As promised, here is the information you wanted." Do the same with phone calls, appointments, returning things to friends, etc. Emphasize that you are a person of your word and watch the respect people have for you grow. Emphasizing your integrity and remembering each and every promise you make—no matter how small— is a powerful combo that will turn integrity into a habit.

Integrity is an *essential* tool for success in all areas of your life. If you aren't trusted or respected, you won't get very far in anything you do. Decide now to always keep your integrity switch in the on position—make it a habit. You'll immediately begin attracting opportunities, improving your relationships and feeling good about your actions. If you want to become an integrity all-star, learn to **underpromise and overdeliver**. This is a motto of the ultrasuccessful. Make it your own.

The Successful Habits
FORMULA

This proven three-step formula has changed the lives of thousands of people—professionals, entrepreneurs, athletes, artists and students. You can use it to change any behaviors that are unproductive, especially ones that may be sabotaging your opportunities for a successful future.

Words of Wisdom from LES:
One of our clients had the habit of always being late for meetings and appointments. He was in the real estate business and his tardiness frustrated people, so much so that he started losing deals. Obviously concerned, he asked me how he could fix the situation. I suggested he throw away all of his business cards and print a new batch, only this time to add the letters A.O.T. after his name. He looked puzzled.

I said: "People will be curious about the letters and will ask what they stand for—Always On Time!" He followed through with the idea, and by the end of the year his income had doubled! His clients appreciated his new level of accountability and were happy to refer him to their friends and family. One new habit changed everything.

1. Identify bad habits and their long-term consequences

Think of all the areas of your life where your actions don't produce the results you want. Make a list of these bad habits and write them down on page 117. You will be using them later in the Action Steps as you transform them into successful habits. Here are a few examples to pull from:

- leaving studying and homework to the last minute

- excessive partying

- seldom visiting the gym and exercising

- overusing your credit card, especially for unnecessary purchases

- breaking small promises

- taking more than you give

- forgetting to floss

- rarely helping clean your house or dorm

- frequently being late for class

- not eating a good breakfast

- hitting the snooze button for an hour every morning

- not doing the dishes the same day you use them

- neglecting to thank your parents and friends for the things they do for you

- constantly forgetting to pay your cell phone bill on time

- allowing instant messaging to distract you from important school work

We beg you, take the time to do this exercise. If you don't write your bad habits down, you will run the risk of blindly going through life totally unaware that some of these bad habits could be leading you into a major crisis. One day you'll wake up and say: "How did this happen to me?" Life will simply observe your calamity and respond, "Another poor victim who never stopped to think—how sad!"

When you define a bad habit, make sure to jot down the long-term consequences that could occur if you don't change this behavior (you will get to do this in the Action Steps). If the consequences are severe, it will be much easier to make a positive change.

If you are unsure of your bad habits, ask a few trusted friends to give you some feedback. **Note: your outward behavior is the truth, whereas your inner perception of your behavior is often an illusion.**

In other words, what you see versus what others see might be *entirely* different. Seek and be open to feedback—it is the key to discovering the type of person you currently are, so you can start becoming the person you really want to be. Have you determined your unproductive habits and jotted them down on page 117? If so, you're ready for step #2.

> *A nail is driven out by another nail.*
> *Habit is overcome by habit.*
>
> —Desiderius Erasmus

2. Define your successful habit and its benefits

Often this is the opposite of your bad habit. For example, if your bad habit is always being late for class, your new successful habit may read, "Always being five minutes early for class." No blindfolds, no pulling rabbits out of hats. It's just that simple.

When you have clearly defined what your new successful habit is, take a few minutes to write down the long-term rewards and benefits this new habit will provide. Continuing the example above, your benefits might read, "Not annoying my professor, not missing any announcements and getting to choose any seat in the room." Hold your enthusiasm. You'll get a chance to do this in the Action Steps.

3. Create a three-part action plan and choose a start date

Your three-part action plan is the catalyst that will transform this new behavior into reality. This is where the rubber meets the road. Will you simply dream about your new habit, or will you create an action plan to adopt it? Don't forget to include a start date. Once you do this, you'll be off to the races.

Before you enter the Action Steps and begin transforming your bad habits into successful habits, there is one critically important point—the only way to ensure your new behavior becomes a well-established habit is to create a **No Exceptions Policy.**

This means that if you decide to exercise three times a week to keep in shape, make sure it's three times, not once or twice. Don't sabotage your good intentions. The reason most people fail when it comes to creating better habits is because they quit or do a half-assed job. Be different—hang in there until the new behavior is a habit. The most difficult stage is the first few weeks. Eventually it becomes easy and you'll do it without thinking. Most habits take between 21 and 30 occurrences before they become part of your new normal behavior.

Throughout the remaining chapters of this book you will learn some of the greatest success principles in the world. Mastering The Successful Habits Formula will ensure a smooth transition for implementing these timeless fundamental strategies.

CONCLUSION

Habits are responsible for up to 90 percent of your behavior and consequently your success, or lack of it.

Successful People Have Successful Habits
- College can be the breeding ground for great habits, or it can spawn an outbreak of bad habits
- The results of your bad habits often don't show up in your life until much later

Successful Habits for Students
1. Always find the answers—create question pages in your notebook and periodically get those questions answered
2. Review your notes—adopt the habit of 4.0 students and review your notes the same day
3. Plan, don't cram—get a day-planner to reduce the stress of forgetting important due dates
4. Synergy—find a study buddy to work with
5. Live by your customized study system—take the risk to test drive different study systems; find the one that works best and use it consistently to get optimal results
6. Insights & Ideas book—use an Insights & Ideas book to capture meaningful ideas or insights

The Ultimate Habit
- Integrity means doing what you say and doing it on time
- Recognize when your integrity switch is off

The Successful Habits Formula
- Step 1—Identify your bad habit and its long-term consequence
- Step 2—Define your new successful habit and its benefits
- Step 3—Create a three-part action plan for replacing your bad habit with your new successful one

---

It's time to eliminate some of your bad habits and create new successful ones. Are you up for the challenge?

ACTION STEPS

Online version available in *The Focus Zone* at:
www.focusedstudent.com

Be a Top Performer

Integrity Check-up

Define Your Bad Habits

The Successful Habits Formula

Be a Top Performer in School

Refer back to page 101 and choose one of the six study habits that interest you the most—always find the answers, review your notes, plan, don't cram, synergy, Insights & Ideas book. Describe below the next three steps you will take to implement this habit. Remember to include the start date.

1. _____

_____

2. _____

_____

3. _____

_____

Start Date: _____

READER/CUSTOMER CARE SURVEY

We care about your opinions! Please take a moment to fill out our online Reader Survey at **http://survey.hcibooks.com**.

As a **"THANK YOU"** you will receive a **VALUABLE INSTANT COUPON** towards future book purchases as well as a **SPECIAL GIFT** available only online! Or, you may mail this card back to us and we will send you a copy of our exciting catalog with your valuable coupon inside.

(PLEASE PRINT IN ALL CAPS)

First Name _____ MI. _____ Last Name _____

Address _____ City _____

State _____ Zip _____ Email _____

1. Gender
- ❑ Female
- ❑ Male

2. Age
- ❑ 8 or younger
- ❑ 9-12
- ❑ 13-16
- ❑ 17-20
- ❑ 21-30
- ❑ 31+

3. Did you receive this book as a gift?
- ❑ Yes
- ❑ No

4. Annual Household Income
- ❑ under $25,000
- ❑ $25,000 - $34,999
- ❑ $35,000 - $49,999
- ❑ $50,000 - $74,999
- ❑ over $75,000

5. What are the ages of the children living in your house?
- ❑ 0 - 14
- ❑ 15+

6. Marital Status
- ❑ Single
- ❑ Married
- ❑ Divorced
- ❑ Widowed

7. How did you find out about the book?
(please choose one)
- ❑ Recommendation
- ❑ Store Display
- ❑ Online
- ❑ Catalog/Mailing
- ❑ Interview/Review

8. Where do you usually buy books?
(please choose one)
- ❑ Bookstore
- ❑ Online
- ❑ Book Club/Mail Order
- ❑ Price Club (Sam's Club, Costco's, etc.)
- ❑ Retail Store (Target, Wal-Mart, etc.)

9. What subject do you enjoy reading about the most?
(please choose one)
- ❑ Parenting/Family
- ❑ Relationships
- ❑ Recovery/Addictions
- ❑ Health/Nutrition
- ❑ Christianity
- ❑ Spirituality/Inspiration
- ❑ Business Self-help
- ❑ Women's Issues
- ❑ Sports

10. What attracts you most to a book?
(please choose one)
- ❑ Title
- ❑ Cover Design
- ❑ Author
- ❑ Content

TAPE IN MIDDLE; DO NOT STAPLE

BUSINESS REPLY MAIL
FIRST-CLASS MAIL PERMIT NO 45 DEERFIELD BEACH, FL

POSTAGE WILL BE PAID BY ADDRESSEE

Health Communications, Inc.
3201 SW 15th Street
Deerfield Beach FL 33442-9875

FOLD HERE

Comments

Integrity Check-up

Name one thing you currently do that could weaken your integrity. Be specific. (Example: telling people I will call them, then forgetting.)

_____

_____

What are you prepared to do to prevent this from jeopardizing your relationships and respect levels? (Examples: tell people to call me rather than saying I will call them, writing down any and all promises I make.)

_____

_____

Define Your Bad Habits

Make a list of all your bad and unproductive habits. Be honest. Remember, awareness is the first step to progress.

_____

_____

_____

_____

_____

_____

_____

The Successful Habits Formula

From your list of bad habits, which ones are holding you back the most? Use the charts below to follow The Successful Habits Formula and transform these bad habits into successful ones. If you are a real keener and want to see more exciting changes in your life, continue this process for the other bad habits you listed above.

Habit That Is Holding Me Back	Successful New Habit	Three-Step Action Plan To Jump-Start My New Habit
EXAMPLE: Not eating breakfast.	Make a fruit and yogurt shake every day before I go to school.	1. Buy frozen fruit from grocery store 2. Set morning alarm 10 minutes earlier 3. Make a shake every day next week—no exceptions
Consequences if Continued	**Specific Benefits**	
- being a zombie in morning classes - wasting money on snacks at school	- more attentive and productive in morning - spend less money on snacks - healthier, more energy	**Start Date:** Monday, October 5

Habit That Is Holding Me Back	Successful New Habit	Three-Step Action Plan To Jump-Start My New Habit
		1. 2.
Consequences if Continued	**Specific Benefits**	3.
		Start Date:

Habit That Is Holding Me Back	Successful New Habit	Three-Step Action Plan To Jump-Start My New Habit
		1.
		2.
Consequences if Continued	Specific Benefits	3.
		Start Date:

Habit That Is Holding Me Back	Successful New Habit	Three-Step Action Plan To Jump-Start My New Habit
		1.
		2.
Consequences if Continued	Specific Benefits	3.
		Start Date:

Fail To Plan, Plan To Fail

If you don't design your own life plan, chances are you'll fall into someone else's plan. Guess what they may have planned for you? Not much!

—Jim Rohn

Jenna isn't called lucky just for having her own swanky apartment.

After graduating from the University of Wisconsin with a finance degree, Jenna Fitzpatrick walked straight into a six-figure salary. She is now being groomed for an executive position at her company. Her journey through academia followed the typical "good student" route—B+ average, extracurricular involvement, internships and a keen interest in learning. The peculiar thing is that many of Jenna's fellow finance friends could also be classified as good students, some even excellent students, yet none of them are making even close to six-figure incomes, nor are they being groomed for an executive position.

Why Jenna? Why not Jack, Joe, Jerome, Jill or Jessica?

When we asked Jenna why she thought she got the job instead of her peers, she said, "I had the skills and experience the investment firm was looking for. I also had a few connections that got me in the door."

We probed a little deeper: "And how did you do that?"

"In my junior year I determined that investment banking was what I wanted to do. I realized that it was a tough field to get into, so I started asking a lot of questions to figure out what I needed to do. Then I worked backwards to ensure I had all the bases covered by the time I graduated."

By Jenna's senior year she had interned at an investment banking firm, volunteered with a student investment club, and had gone to various trade shows and conferences. So although Jenna's friends think she has the luck of the Irish, what Jenna really had was a solid plan, a plan that ensured she developed the skills, experience and contacts needed to land a kick-ass investment banker job—her ultimate career choice.

The phenomenon of luck has been around for a long time. However, those who appear to be lucky know that luck is more often solid planning in disguise. Jenna is a prime example of this. Luck was not the root of her success after college; it was a well-executed plan. People like Jenna are not super-human, nor are they more intelligent than everyone else; they are regular individuals who have a plan that takes them where they want to go.

ANDREW:
It always confused me when people called me the L word . . . lucky that is. I would usually just smile and shrug it off, but in my head I was thinking YOU COULD HAVE DONE THIS TOO!

This happened most while I was doing exchange programs in Southeast Asia and Europe. Lucky became a common theme in e-mails and instant messages. When my classmates dropped the L bomb it really made me wonder why they didn't grant themselves "lucky" by participating in these exciting exchange programs as well.

Luck is preparation meeting opportunity.

—Oprah Winfrey

Have you ever admired someone else's luck? If you have, ask yourself if it's possible for you to do what that person has done—a trip to Europe, interning at a cool company or landing a sweet job. After investigating the steps and strategies that person took, ask yourself whether you, too, could have had the same luck if you had followed a similar plan.

Begin With the End
IN MIND

If you take a frog and drop it into a pot of sizzling hot water, what will the frog do? Jump out! The frog instantly dislikes where it is and makes a quick decision to leap for its life. If you take the same frog (or another one if the first got away), place it in a pot of cold water, then put the pot on the stove and heat it slowly, what happens? The frog hangs out for awhile, enjoying its new hot tub . . . and soon enough you'll be serving frog legs to your neighbor's cat. There is actually a moral to this story—keep reading to find out what it is.

The first step in creating a plan is understanding your destination, your endpoint. Begin with the end in mind. The problem is that most students never take the time to figure out what destination interests them. Students who get sucked into the cycle of everyday college life—never taking the time to think about where they want to end up—will feel the heat in their last couple of years when important decisions about their future need to be made. For instance, look at Nick Holdstrom from Washington State.

Like many other students, Nick had good grades in high school.

He had no trouble being accepted into his local college. He was looking forward to his new life as a student and didn't really think about a career. His father owned a successful welding business and regarded himself as a hardworking blue-collar guy. He was proud that Nick would be the first in the family to bring home a degree, and he figured that Nick would find his own career niche with the help of all those worldly professors. Nick's older buddies had given him a picture of college being party central for the first two years. "Enjoy yourself," they said. "You can study hard later."

Now three years have whizzed by. Nick is in his senior year and still has no clue about what direction to head in or what career he is interested in. His most admired skill is the speed at which he can shotgun a beer—not something employers typically look for. Nick is starting to feel the heat, especially from his parents. Like the poor little frog, Nick didn't feel the heat creeping up as he got comfortable in the college routine, never taking the time to think about where he wanted to end up. Now the pot is boiling. Nick has big decisions to make about his future and little time to make them.

Without a vision of where you are going, it's difficult to get there. By reading Focusing Strategy #2—*Ignite The Fire Within*, and starting to fill in your Passion Puzzle™ you now have a better understanding of what type of work will give you passion. Focusing Strategy #3—*Are You Heading in the Right Direction?* gave you a better understanding of what direction is best for you. Combined, these two make up your ultimate career—the end to always have in mind. Keep this picture front and center, constantly. If the picture is a bit blurry, it might be because you whizzed through the Action Steps. This is the most important part of this book—it is your future career at stake.

By filling in your Passion Puzzle™ and determining what direction is best for you, you will know where you are heading and can begin planning accordingly. Yes, this takes a bit of time and investigation, but how nice will it be to really *know* what career you want to pursue? Skipping this step will make it tough to make decisions about your major, about what jobs to work in during summer breaks and about what type of experience you need to land a decent job after graduating. Go back to the Action Steps in Focusing Strategies #2 and #3 if you need to clarify your career picture. If you already have a decent understanding of an ultimate career or two, then you are ready to rock on to the next section and create a bulletproof plan that will accelerate your progress.

Build Your
CREDENTIALS

In the game of life there are passengers and there are drivers. If you want to choose where you end up, strap yourself into the driver's seat. You are about to learn how to create a powerful plan that will take you where you want to go.

A concrete plan serves as a blueprint, helping you custom-build the life you want during and after college. Having this blueprint gives you a feeling of being in control. You are the ultimate designer, builder and implementer of your own destiny. Nobody else can do it for you. Many students go through college flying by the seat of their pants, making important decisions on a whim. Consequently, they end up somewhere they don't want to be. You have two options:

1. Take control of your own life and create your own plan.
2. Fall into someone else's plan and see where you end up.

It really is *your* choice.

LUC:
The summer before I headed off to university, I landed my first office job. I envisioned a corner office, a comfy chair and a beautiful view of the downtown core. Imagine my dismay when my office ended up being the mailroom, which didn't even have a window. All my friends were partying, working at golf courses and enjoying the beautiful summer weather while I was confined to a tiny, cluttered mailroom.

I was the office mail boy, or as my coworker used to call me, the office mail bitch. The name was fitting, because all I did was bitch. Rather than coming in early, staying late and working my butt off, I came to work tired and spent more time on my cell phone than delivering mail. At the end of the summer I was given a performance review, and it was far from excellent. As a result I learned two very important lessons.

The first was that I never wanted to be a mail boy again. The second was realizing that the longer I did a mediocre job as the office mail boy, the longer I would be one. There was no cozy elevator to the top. If I had given my all and shown potential, I could have been relieved of the mail boy duties a lot sooner.

During your college years you have three to five summer breaks to test your interests and build your credentials—risk free. What a deal!

> There is no such thing as dead-end jobs,
> only dead-end attitudes.

The activities you engage in during your summers will contribute greatly to the opportunities, or lack of opportunities, you have when you graduate. There are two ways you can approach your summer jobs:

1. Find a job that will give you good experience, and use this experience to get an even better job the next summer.

2. Search for the highest paying job to help offset your high tuition bills.

If you choose option one (and it is *your* choice), you will have a much better job in the following years and you will be closer to, or working in, your ultimate career when you graduate. Sound good? Building your credentials this way is important. It's also a lot simpler when you have a plan, as shown in the following chart.

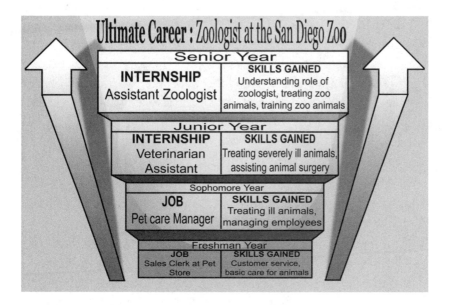

Building your credentials in the work world is like going to grade school. To enter grade two, you must first pass grade one. To pass grade one you need to prove you have the skills to take on grade two. Obviously, the sooner you pass grade one the sooner you will be in grade six—where you can boss around the grade fives, fours, threes, twos and ones!

A four-step method for determining where to work during summer break:

1. What skills does your ultimate career require?

2. How many of these skills have you currently mastered or acquired?

3. What skills do you still need to develop?

4. What job will provide those skills?

The principle of building your credentials is nothing new. You are in college because you (or someone else) has identified that you don't know everything. The key is to build the *right* credentials so you move closer to where you want to be. An aspiring actress working at an accounting firm is a good example of building the wrong credentials.

> *I don't think much of a man who*
> *is not wiser today than he was yesterday.*
>
> —Abraham Lincoln

Summer jobs and internships are not the only ways to build great credentials. With the experience-focused mindset you will naturally build credentials through extracurricular activities, international exchanges and innovative programs as well.

© The Power of Focus, 2005. CASEY JOHNSON

"Dear Santa: For Christmas this year I want communication skills, analytical-reasoning ability, proficiency in neurolinguistic programming, and a participatory leadership style . . ."

Mo Money,
MO PROBLEMS

If you intend to look (or are currently looking) for summer jobs that pay well because you want to offset your high tuition bills, read the following carefully.

It's hard to say no to a good-paying job, especially when you are a broke student living in a status-oriented society and consumed with impressing the opposite sex. Unfortunately, seeking a high-paying job while you are in college can *prevent* you from receiving an even higher-paying job when you graduate. How come?

The following story shows how one student went from "big bling" to almost broke . . . but attests that it was the best thing he ever did.

Tyler Irving started his college business program with the typical degree-focused mindset.
"I wanted to get my degree as quickly as possible," he says. "I thought it was my ticket to bigger and better things." On his first summer break, Tyler headed home. "I went home to work for my dad. The job was hard labor, but it paid great! The next year I did the same thing—eight months of studying and four months working for my dad."

During two summers Tyler made more than $28,000. Not bad for a student in his first years of college. However, Tyler was missing out on something he couldn't afford to overlook.

"Late in my junior year it hit me. Working labor jobs every summer wasn't giving me the experience I needed to succeed in business. I only had a year and a half left to develop the skills and contacts I needed to get a good job." Tyler wasn't completely certain about what he wanted to do, but he did have an interest in the stock market. Tyler soon found two great opportunities: one was to run for the VP finance position of a business club on campus and the other was to work as an intern for an investment firm for the summer. There was just one little problem—the salary from the internship was a big fat zero. Tyler's summer salary had been eliminated, and the VP finance position was volunteer work so his cash-flow was tight.

"Taking on some debt was the only way I could take advantage of these opportunities and still survive financially the following year. It was damn scary at first, but I quickly realized that the debt I was incurring was for a good cause—it was allowing me to develop the skills and experience I needed to succeed after college."

In his last year of school, success became synonymous with Tyler's name. He loved working at the investment firm, made amazing contacts through the business club and had exciting job offers with salaries more than double that of his laboring job. "Taking the huge pay cut in college was tough at first, but it turned out to be the best decision I have ever made."

Remember, the choice is yours; you can either work to earn or work to learn. Tracking the success of past graduates proves that those who work to *learn* create future financial payoffs that far exceed the short-term benefit of those working to *earn*. College is one time in your life when being broke is acceptable. Embrace it while you can, and give yourself permission to work for the experience, not for the paycheck. Don't worry. After reading Focusing Strategy #8—*Your Financial Future Starts NOW,* you will know how to manage money and how to make it work for you so you never have to worry about it again.

> Every job, every course and every role
> you play should take you one step
> closer to your ultimate career.

Are you heading in the Self-employed/ Business Owner or Artist Direction?
TAKE NOTE:

Even though you may not be applying for a job after graduation, building your credentials and beginning with the end in mind is equally important.

To be successful in these directions you need experience, and college is the perfect time to acquire it.

Every job you work is an exchange of your time for something in return. Receiving only a paycheck in return for your time is a crummy deal. Don't sell yourself short! Exchange your time for the knowledge, contacts and experience that are priceless in comparison to a paycheck.

Creating A Bulletproof
PLAN

Have you ever made a wish? Perhaps at Christmas while tugging on a cracker? Or while throwing a penny into a fountain? Or maybe when you saw a shooting star in the night sky? At one time or another everyone has wished for something outrageous: a million dollars, a trip around the world, or a date with the cute guy or gal from class. What wishes have you made? Wishing is exciting because for a brief moment you are taken outside the boundaries of everyday life and given the chance to desire anything you please.

Wishes form a gateway into your reality. They are important because they stimulate your mind and give you a great reason to step outside your comfort zone. However, they are not the concrete building blocks that are needed in a plan. Goals are those concrete building blocks. They are the milestones you set that make your wishes come true.

> *If you're bored with life—you don't get up
> every morning with a burning desire to do things
> —you don't have enough goals.*
>
> —Lou Holtz

What exactly is a goal? Everyone has heard the buzzword "goal" from a professor or a parent, but what really *is* a goal?

Join the 3% Club

A study done in 1953 at Yale University found that only 3 percent of the graduating class had written goals.

After 20 years, the same 3 percent were wealthier than the other 97 percent combined!

Will you write down your goals?
Will you be in the 3% of your graduating class?

Goals quantify your wishes. They provide motivation and a path to achievement. Setting and achieving goals is what keeps you moving forward. Goals are the fuel necessary to keep your engine running, the map that will guide you to where you want to be. Imagine planning a road trip to Mexico and having no map and no gas in the car—how far would you get?

Consider the alternative to setting goals—just drifting along aimlessly, hoping that one day good fortune will fall into your lap. Wake up! You'd have a better chance finding a grain of sugar on a sandy beach. Goals will allow you to accomplish anything you desire, if you know the smart way to go about it.

The SMART
GOAL SYSTEM

In the work world you will be bombarded with acronyms. To get you warmed up, here is an acronym for setting goals —SMART.

S is for Specific
A goal must be specific. Wishy-washy goals are too easily lost in the busyness of college life. Here are a few examples of wishy-washy goals:

- I'm going to eat healthier.

- I'm going to spend less money.

- I'm going to study more this semester.

- I'm going to start volunteering.

Great, but how? Your love handles aren't going to fall off on their own. Set goals that are **specific**.

Specific means explicitly defined with boundaries and ranges. On what days, and for how long, are you going to the gym this week? Are you going to tone your arms, build a six pack or tighten up the old rump? The specifics provide visuals that allow you to know immediately when you are meeting your goals and when you are off track.

M is for Measurable
"I will be nicer to my roommate everyday this week." Maybe you will, maybe you won't. You will never know because this feeble attempt at a goal is not measurable. When a

goal is measurable you can track your progress towards achieving it. If it's not measurable, it's too easy to get off track and achieve nothing.

> A goal that is not specific and measurable is just a slogan.

The test: Ask yourself, "Can someone else measure whether or not I achieved my goal?" If the answer is no, your goal is not measurable.

A is for Attainable

Sad as it may be, some things are not attainable. If you are four feet tall and have poor hand-eye coordination, a basketball career in the NBA by next month, next year or even next century is probably out of reach. There is a fine line, however, between a big aggressive goal and one that is unattainable.

The easiest way to take a chunk out of your self-esteem and self-confidence is to set an unattainable goal, then beat yourself up for not achieving it.

The test: If you are relying on a miracle to achieve your goal (growing three feet or having 34 hours in a day) it is unattainable. Keep your goals realistic and watch your confidence build as you accomplish them.

R is for Reason

R is the most important letter in the word SMART. For a goal to be reached you must have a strong reason to want to reach it. Your reason becomes the fuel that keeps you moving toward your goal—the motivation, the inspiration, the kick in the butt you need to continue striving for it. Be sure that each and every goal you set includes the reason why you want to achieve it. Doing this will drastically increase your odds of achieving any goal you set.

The test: Ask yourself, "What is my reason for setting this goal? Is it strong enough to push me into action and keep me going when times get tough?"

T is for Time-Stamped

A time stamp on your goal means that on a specific day, at a specific time, it expires. A time stamp is enormously important because, let's face it, most students are expert procrastinators (we will tackle this thorny issue in the next focusing strategy). As a result of procrastination, tasks do not get done until days, hours or minutes before they are due. If there is no due date, they won't get done at all. A time stamp prevents you from dabbling around your goals and greatly increases the likelihood that you will accomplish them.

> A goal without a time stamp is like a check
> without a signature—it has no value.

The test: Ask yourself, "At what specific time in the future will I know if I have accomplished this goal?" If you do not have an answer, you need a time stamp.

S	– Specific
M	– Measurable
A	– Attainable
R	– Reason
T	– Time-Stamped

If a goal is SMRT or ART or SAT or SMAT or AT or any other combination of S-M-A-R-T that does not have five letters, you are seriously diminishing the possibility of ever achieving that goal.

The Semester
SYSTEM

How often should you set goals? There is no one-size-fits-all answer, but in the college world it makes sense to take advantage of the semester system. Every semester you have different classes, professors, roommates and maybe a newly refined set of interests and ambitions. Setting goals at the beginning of the semester is the single most powerful way to put your plan for that semester into motion.

LUC:
Because I was in an intensive co-op program, I moved 19 times while at college (never because of roommate rumbles, but thanks for asking). Every semester was a brand new adventure. I would sit down a week before the start of a

new semester, assess my current progress and determine what I wanted to accomplish for the next semester. Then I'd set goals for the semester—what mark I wanted to get in each course, how many days a week I would work out and how many parties I was going to throw. Setting goals was easy because every goal automatically had a time stamp —the end of the semester. All I had to do was ensure my goals were specific, measurable, attainable and existed for a good reason.

BONUS: By having goals for each semester, any big (or small) decisions you face during the semester become much easier. When faced with a decision, simply refer back to your goals and choose the option that moves you closer to accomplishing them. Sound easy? It is! Don't let indecision cause you stress and anxiety. Use goals to guide your decisions and actions.

Areas of life to set goals
It wouldn't be fair to leave you hanging, withholding the important areas of your life in which goals are needed. Here they are, along with some SMART examples.

SCHOOL:
- I will finish this semester with a B average or higher
  because I need a B to get accepted into the education faculty.

HEALTH & FITNESS:
- I am going to lose at least 10 pounds by the end of the semester
  because I want to feel better about how I look.

PERSONAL:
- I will read a book for fun each month to relax and to help
  prevent me from getting sick due to stress.

FINANCIAL:
- I will only use my cell phone on evenings and weekends so my
  bills this semester are less than $40 per month.

FUN TIME:
- I will go to Daytona Beach for spring break because I will always regret it if I don't.

RELATIONSHIPS:
- I will attend three events put on by the marketing club, so I can meet more friends who share the same interests as me.

CONTRIBUTION:
- I am going to volunteer at the homeless shelter for a few hours every Thursday this semester because I am blessed with the opportunities I have and I want to give back.

Don't miss out on the Action Steps at the end of this focusing strategy where you can begin setting SMART goals in all of these key areas.

I am so smart, S–M–R–T.

—Homer Simpson

Goals keep you focused and heading toward the things you want in life. However, sometimes the things you want may seem out of reach or impossible (like getting accepted into law school, becoming a movie star or making a million dollars a year). The next section will show you a powerful way to make anything within your reach.

Your Success Mechanism

According to Charlie Tremendous Jones, "Everyone has a success mechanism and a failure mechanism. The failure mechanism goes off by itself. The success mechanism only goes off with a goal. Every time we write down and talk about a goal we push the button to start the success mechanism."

Thinking
BIG

Our friend Jack Canfield, co-creator of the phenomenally successful *Chicken Soup for the Soul* series, tells this story about an ambitious young man.

Monty was the son of a wandering horse trainer.
He would go from stable to stable, race track to race track, farm to farm and ranch to ranch, training horses. As a result, the boy's high school career was continually interrupted. When he was a senior, he was asked to write a paper about what he wanted to be and do when he grew up.

That night he wrote a seven-page paper describing his goal of someday owning a horse ranch. He wrote about his dream in great detail and he even drew a diagram of a 200-acre ranch, showing the location of all the buildings, the stables and the track. Then he drew a detailed floor plan for a 4,000-square-foot house that would sit on his 200-acre dream ranch.

He put a great deal of his heart into the project, and the next day he handed it to his teacher with pride. Two days later he received his paper back. On the front page was a large red F with a note that read, "See me after class."

The boy with the big vision went to see the teacher after class and asked, "Why did I receive an F?"

The teacher said, "This is an unrealistic dream for a young boy like you. You have no money. You come from a poor family. You have no resources. Owning a horse ranch requires a lot of money. You have to buy the land. You have to pay for the original breeding stock, and later you'll have to pay large stud fees. There's no way you can ever do it." Then the teacher added, "If you will rewrite this paper with a more realistic goal, I will reconsider your grade." The boy went home and thought about it long and hard. He asked his father what he should do. His father said, "Look, son, you have to make up your own mind on this. However, I think it is a very important decision for you."

Finally, after sitting with it for a week, the boy turned in the same paper, making no changes at all. He told his teacher, "You can keep the F and I'll keep my dream."

Years later, Monty Roberts, the young man who had stood up to his teacher, was sharing his story with a youth-at-risk group in his home. He concluded by saying: "I tell you this story because you are all sitting in my 4,000-square-foot house in the middle of my 200-acre horse ranch. I still have that school paper framed over the fireplace." He added, "The best part of the story is that two summers ago that same school teacher brought 30 kids to camp out on my ranch for a week. When the teacher was leaving, he said, 'Look, Monty, I can tell you this now. When I was your teacher, I was something of a dream stealer. During those years I stole a lot of kids' dreams. Fortunately you had enough gumption not to give up on yours.' "

The message is clear: Think big and believe big is possible!

> *If you are going to be thinking anyway,*
> *you might as well think big.*

—Donald Trump

Like Monty, most kids see the world as their oyster and nothing, absolutely nothing, is outside of their reach. As we grow older, however, our big dreams begin to get shut down, and we are led to believe that they are no longer possible. Maybe it was the playground bully with stabbing statements like, "Nice try loser, you suck!" Or perhaps disapproval from your parents, who have also had their dreams stripped away and now work at jobs that give them little fulfillment. Are you willing to let others decide your capabilities? Or will you do as Monty did and prove that you can accomplish anything you truly desire despite less-than-perfect circumstances?

"Timmy and Tommy were always looking
for the next big thing."

Do you want to achieve big things? A big house, a big car, a big vacation, a big job, a big bank account and a big impact on the world? Who wouldn't! The only thing that makes these big things seem out of reach are the limits imposed on you by others and yourself. Fortunately there is a simple technique for overcoming these imposed limitations and regaining your childhood ambitions. Here it is:

Relax and focus for a moment. Visualize your life 10 years from now in all of its various components: work, relationships, finances, health and personal accomplishments. Take your time and really envision it. Got it? Okay, now take what you see and make it twice as big—twice as extravagant, twice as large, twice as expensive, twice as high profile.

Can you see it? How do you feel? It's exciting, isn't it? Is your new vision possible? Sure it is, and you're already on your way there because you just took the first step—visualizing it.

Back in 1987, while struggling as a comic, Jim Carrey practiced this very activity. Often he'd drive his beat-up old car to Mulholland Drive in the Hollywood hills to visualize his future. While gazing over the city of Los Angeles one afternoon, he wrote himself a check for "Acting Services Rendered" in the amount of $10 million. He dated it for Thanksgiving 1995. He carried this check with him at all times and continued visualizing his big dreams. By 1995, Carrey was making $20 million per movie and had signed the old check for $10 million over to his dad.

Take a few minutes to capture your big vision each and every day. Remember, don't let others shut down your vision. Keep focusing on it and soon it will unfold into an exciting reality.

Shoot for the moon. Even if you miss,
you'll land among the stars.

—Les Brown

Eliminate the word "impossible" from your vocabulary. It takes no additional effort to think big than it does to think small. **No one accomplishes more than they set out to do, so set out to accomplish big things.**

CONCLUSION

It's simple: A solid plan is essential to getting what you want in life.

Luck is Solid Planning in Disguise
- Where you end up is the direct outcome of your actions.
- With a little planning and good execution of that plan, anyone can be deemed lucky.

Begin with the End in Mind
- Without a vision of where you are going it will be hard to ever get there.

Build Your Credentials
- Every job, every course and every role you play should take you one step closer to where you want to be.
- Work to learn, not to earn.

Wishes
- Wishes have no boundaries and no rules. A wish opens the mind to infinite possibilities.

Goals
- Goals are the building blocks of a solid plan and are what turn wishes into reality.
- Set goals every semester that are Specific, Measurable, Attainable, reinforce a Reason and Time-stamped.
- Set SMART goals in the following areas: school, health, personal, financial, fun time, relationships and contribution.

Thinking Big
- If you visualize what you want, it will soon unfold into an exciting reality.
- No one accomplishes more than they set out to do, so set out to do big things.

Now it's time to buckle your seatbelt! You are about to do some very important Action Steps that will drive you toward your ultimate career.

ACTION STEPS

Online version available in *The Focus Zone* at:
www.focusedstudent.com

Building Your Credentials

Wish List

Setting SMART Goals

Building Your Credentials

What skills will you need to land your ultimate career? What roles will provide these skills? Using the space below, brainstorm a list of these roles and the accompanying skills you will gain. A role will likely be a summer job or an internship, but don't stop there; it can also be an overseas exchange or a volunteer position.

Skills will be things like: managing people, technical writing, sales and leadership. After a quick brainstorm use the chart on the next page to create an action plan. If you would like an example, flip to page 127. If you have forgotten what your ultimate career is, flip to page 90 for ideas.

_____   _____

_____   _____

_____   _____

_____   _____

Ultimate Career :_____

Senior Year	
Role:_____	Skills to be Gained

Junior Year	
Role:_____	Skills to be Gained

Sophomore Year	
Role:_____	Skills to be Gained

Freshman Year	
Role:_____	Skills to be Gained

Your Customized Wish List

Before you read any further, put on your creative hat and remove the word "impossible" from your vocabulary.

There are two ways you can complete this Action Step:

1. Go to *The Focus Zone* at www.focusedstudent.com and do it online. This online version will allow you to pick and drag from an extensive list of exciting wishes. This method will be easier and take less time. It is also printer-friendly so you can post it on your wall.

2. Pull out a piece of blank paper and make two columns: College Wishes and Life Wishes. Under College Wishes write any wishes you have while you are a student. Under Life Wishes write wishes you want to accomplish before you are 100 years old. Write down anything! There are no rules, no guidelines and anything goes, so wish BIG. Here's an example to get you started.

COLLEGE WISHES	LIFE WISHES
Run a marathon	Travel to Europe
Type 60 words per minute	Swim with dolphins
Spring break in Mexico	Learn to speak Spanish
Be president of a club	Have my own TV show
Study abroad	Have children
Work on a school newspaper	Ride in a submarine
Compete internationally	Climb Mount Everest

Always be adding to your wish lists—they are a never-ending work in progress. Wish lists contain things you would like to do or wish to do—they are *not* goals.

Setting SMART Goals

You have now identified the credentials your ultimate career requires and the wishes you have for your life. In this Action Step you will set SMART goals to ensure your credentials actually get built and that your wishes will be met.

This Action Step can also be completed in two ways:

OPTION 1:
Go to *The Focus Zone* at *www.focusedstudent.com* and do it online. This online versiongives you more space, more examples and can be printed in a sexy format.

OPTION 2:
Use the chart on the following page and fill in the blank column.

Set goals for this semester. It doesn't matter whether you are at the beginning, middle or end of the semester. If you don't start now, you will probably never start. Soon you'll be wondering why your credentials were never built and why your wishes were never met. Start now!

Ensure your goals are **S**pecific, **M**easurable, **A**ttainable, reinforce a **R**eason and **T**ime-stamped. Review what you wrote in the Action Steps above. What can you start working on this semester? For example, if on your Wish List you wrote "*Be elected as president of the geology club,*" and for Building Your Credentials you wrote, "*Intern at an advertising agency,*" then you might set goals like this:

- This semester I will spend 30 minutes with the president of the geology club every week to learn from her successes and increase my chances of being elected next year.

- Before the end of the semester, I will ask three marketing professors if they know of any internships at local advertising agencies to ensure I have the credentials needed to land a fantastic job after graduation.

If you use this process for every semester in college, you will be AMAZED at how many of your wishes and goals come true.

Goal Category	Description	My SMART Goal
* To see a SMART goal example for each category go to page 137.		
SCHOOL	Any overriding goal you have for school or a goal for a specific course	
HEALTH & FITNESS	Anything to do with your personal health and fitness	
PERSONAL	Anything you personally want to have, be or do. Anything spiritual would also be in here	
FINANCIAL	Anything related to budgeting, spending, saving or money in general	
RELATIONSHIPS	Family, professional, friendships, mentors, significant others	
FUN TIME	Vacations, trips, sports, parties, special events	
CONTRIBUTION	Giving back to your community or to others	

Grab The Wheel
& Hit The Gas!

Just do it.

—Nike

If three birds are sitting on a fence and two decide to fly away, how many birds are left?

You may decide on an ultimate career, decide to build your credentials, decide to set goals or decide to take control of your life. You may even decide to fly off a fence, but decisions alone do not guarantee action. If you haven't yet made the connection, there are still three birds sitting on that fence.

The first half of this chapter will show you how to break through the two major roadblocks that prevent most people from taking action—procrastination and fear. The second half will teach you three proven and powerful techniques that will help you get what you want, no matter what. With these crucial tools in your toolbox, nothing can stop you from building your blueprint and implementing your plan.

Roadblock #1
PROCRASTINATION

Do you have a hard time starting essays? Do you leave your studying until the very last minute? Do you ever notice how your house, apartment or dorm room starts getting cleaner around exam time?

Let's face it, students are master procrastinators. A psychologist by the name of William Knaus found that 90 percent of all college students procrastinate, 25 percent being chronic procrastinators who are likely to end up dropping out. Let's look at Sally, a typical college student procrastinating through a typical college day.

Bzzzzzzzz! The dreaded sound of Sally's alarm slaps her awake at 7:00 A.M.

Last night Sally had decided to get up early. She was feeling a little tired and went to bed before finishing her psychology paper. But it's December in New York and the chill of her room makes getting out of bed a feat of courage. Bzzzzzzz . . . smash! At 7:15 A.M. Sally's bed feels even warmer as she drifts back to sleep. It's 9:05 A.M. before Sally finally stumbles out of bed. After checking her e-mail, which leads to reformatting her hard drive (it was running a bit slow), she absolutely has to post pictures from last weekend's party on her website. Now it's 10:50 A.M. Class is in 10 minutes, but Sally's stomach won't let her leave without a quick bite. That's okay, though, Sally's on a granola bar diet and has become used to the eat-'n'-run routine.

Class break at 3:00 P.M. is a perfect time to focus on that psychology assignment before her evening class. Sally chooses to work in the cafeteria. She knows it's a little distracting but rationalizes that eating and studying is a good way to multitask. But just as her pen hits the paper, Jen from drama 101 approaches. More than 24 hours have passed since they last chatted and hearing the latest gossip can't wait.

Sally strolls home around 8:00 P.M. She is feeling quite tired from her busy day and allows herself a 15-minute break to watch TV before finally getting started on her psychology paper. But 15 minutes turns into 50—after all, her roommates are watching her favorite show. Sally starts getting anxious about her paper. It is due tomorrow and worth a lot of marks. On the way to her room, she decides that a quick shower will wake her up and make her more productive. While showering she sees that the bathroom is a little dirty and it is her turn to clean it. Soon it's midnight. Struggling through the second page of her paper, Sally wishes she had started earlier. She is tired and realizes her lack of productivity. At the rate she's going she'll be up all night. She decides to go to bed and wake up early the next morning to finish her paper. Bzzzzzzzz . . . smash!

Procrastination is doing things that bring you immediate pleasure instead of focusing on your priorities. By rationalizing and justifying reasons to do pleasurable activities first, the important things don't get done. Stress soars and the quality of your work goes down. In the end, procrastination prevents you from reaching your goals and leads you into a world of "if only."

- "*If only* I had gained volunteer experience I would have landed that job."

- "*If only* I had studied harder I would have been accepted into law school."

- "*If only* I had tried out for the basketball team I would have made a lot of friends."

- "*If only* I had gone on that exchange program I could have seen the world."

Playing the woulda, coulda, shoulda game will destroy golden opportunities that life brings your way. It's very easy to let four years of procrastination fly by and end up with deep regrets, remorse and guilt, knowing you could have done more.

The pain of discipline weighs ounces
and lasts for moments. The pain of regret
weighs tons and lasts forever.

—Jim Rohn

If you are like most students, you realize your procrastination problem and would love to see it perish. A study conducted by Solomon and Rothblum found that 65 percent of college students want to learn how to stop procrastinating over writing term papers, 62 percent feel the need to study for exams more promptly, and 55 percent hope to read their assignments earlier.

Help has arrived! . . . and no, it doesn't involve attending therapy or a "Procrastinators Anonymous" meeting. The solution isn't a 12-step program, it is four fighting mechanisms to prevent procrastination from eating you alive. What will be your weapon of choice?

Four Ways to Fight
PROCRASTINATION

1. Become mechanical

Have you ever procrastinated about brushing your teeth? We hope not. Brushing your teeth is a mechanical process, a habit performed with little conscious thought. Becoming mechanical is effective because you take action before thinking about whether you like the task, and thus the task gets accomplished pain-free. Think of something you constantly procrastinate about (working out, or getting up when your alarm sounds). Think of a way to make it mechanical (going to the gym every day right after biology class, or getting out of bed at the first sound of the alarm).

A few mechanical processes to get you started:

1. Get up at the FIRST sound of your alarm EVERY morning (or at least after one hit of the snooze button).

2. Study at the SAME time every day (during a class break, right after dinner, etc.).

3. If you think of a question to ask, ask IMMEDIATELY or forever hold your peace.

As you learned in Focusing Strategy #4, you will need to repeat your new mechanical process 20 to 30 times to make it a habit. Once you do, these once-dreaded tasks will be transformed into easy and painless routines.

2. The sausage method
Imagine trying to wolf down a foot-long sausage in one bite. It would be hard to swallow, wouldn't it?

The same goes for assignments. Sitting down to start a 40-page paper is a daunting, hard-to-swallow task. The solution is to break the large task into smaller pieces, or subtasks. Break an essay into outline, introduction, first draft, etc. Divide the task of finding a summer job into update resume, review job postings, ask family and friends, and so on. Small, manageable tasks are less intimidating to get started and easier to complete—and completing them will give you a great sense of accomplishment.

Do you have a large project looming over your head? If so, try chopping it into smaller segments and focusing on one segment at a time. It's like eating the sausage one small bite at a time.

3. The to-do-today list

Every day make a list of all the things you need to do today. Prioritize the list in order of most important to least important. Begin your day with the most important task on the list and do not start the next task until the first is completed. Continue down your list as the day goes on. If something comes up (a friend wants to meet you for coffee, you're given a new math assignment, your car breaks down, etc.) assess its priority, add it to your list where appropriate and attend to it in that order.

IMPORTANT NOTE: Many things will come up throughout the day that appear urgent but really aren't. E-mails are a common culprit. Don't let these tasks that appear urgent prevent you from finishing the tasks of higher priority—stay focused on your most important tasks. By creating this list every day (or at least on your busier days) and working through it in priority order, you will enjoy the confidence that your time is being spent wisely. Furthermore, when you review your list at the end of the day, you'll be amazed at how much you completed. Sleep soundly, guilt-free, and snore all you want as a reward for your accomplishments.

4. Find your reason *why*

Behind every action is a strong reason *why*. Your *why* is what motivates you to act. Why go talk to the International Exchange office? Why study for this exam? Why work for free? Without a reason *why*, these things won't get done.

> *Procrastination is like a credit card:*
> *it's a lot of fun until you get the bill.*

> —Christopher Parker

To create your *why*, look at the bigger picture and see the consequences of your procrastination. Make the negative consequences of your inaction a vivid picture in your mind. For example, you might say to yourself:

- "If I don't talk to the International Exchange office NOW (your procrastination) I might miss an important application deadline that will ultimately prevent me from learning a new language and experiencing new cultures." (the big-picture consequence—your reason *why*)

- "If I put off studying another hour (your procrastination) I will score a lower grade on my chemistry final, which will reduce my GPA along with my chances of getting into medical school." (the big-picture consequence—your reason *why*)

- "If I don't find a way to gain volunteer experience (your procrastination) I will reduce my chance of getting a good summer job. If I work a mediocre summer job, I won't have the experience I need to get the job I want when I graduate." (the big-picture consequence—your reason *why*)

Different types of procrastination will require a different fighting style. Keep yourself armed by remembering the four fighting styles—make it mechanical, the sausage method, your to-do-today list and finding your *why*—and choose the method that stands the best chance against the procrastination villain you are fighting.

ANDREW:
I swear the meter maid was out to get me. If my parking meter had expired by just two minutes—smack!—another ticket under my wiper blade. My collection of tickets was piling up, and I seemed to let it, probably to spite the malicious meter maid. I knew I should pay the fines, but never seemed to get around to it. What a mistake that was. A couple months later the court subpoena arrived.

By that time the collective fines and late charges were enough to push me into starvation for the rest of the semester. Procrastination had gotten the better of me. However, I learned a valuable lesson. I found my reason *why*, the motivation for paying parking tickets on time.

Roadblock #2
FEAR

Like procrastination, fear prevents us from taking action. It is the second major roadblock on the path toward your ultimate career. *Fear Factor* host Joe Rogan watches fear every week as contestants on the popular TV show do outrageous tasks like crawling through pipes of raw sewage, scaling sky-high office towers and eating blended rat soup. If you've watched the show you may have noticed that the winners always have one thing in common—they take immediate action and step into their fear full throttle. This doesn't mean they become fearless, because often they're shaking in their bikinis. However, they accept the situation despite what they feel and give it their all anyway.

The ABCs
OF FEAR

A. Fear does not go away

Believe it or not, no one is fearless. The craziest daredevils of all time will admit that they feel fear before performing a stunt. Even streakers at football games tremble in their tighty whities before baring it all. Fear always exists to some degree. The trick is learning how to manage your fear so it doesn't hinder your progress. Fear is like body odor; it's always going to be with you, but if you learn how to recognize and neutralize it, chances are it won't have a negative effect.

B. Fear stems from uncertainty

All fear develops from an uncertainty that you won't be able to cope with what could happen. Here's a news flash—you can handle ANYTHING! There is no situation in life you cannot handle. You have greater capacity than you realize. Once you come to this realization, you will not be bothered by fear because even in a worst-case scenario you can handle it.

If you are contemplating an exchange program overseas, keep a close eye out for fear attempting to sabotage your plans. These overseas experiences involve many uncertainties—language barriers, weird food, strange living arrangements, etc. Be confident that you can handle these uncertainties, because you can. Surveys have shown that the majority of students who don't study abroad list it among their top regrets after graduation. These are the students who let fear get the better of them and regretted it later, after they realized they could have handled it.

C. Pushing through fear is much easier than living with it

We have all experienced exam anxiety (by the way, anxiety and nervousness are forms of fear). Imagine an exam date that always remains just a few days away and forever living with the anxiety of writing the exam. Wouldn't that suck! By writing the exam we release our fear and feel a great surge of freedom (and often a great urge to pound back a root beer or two). The good thing about exams is that you are forced to act on a specific day at a specific time. However, other things that make you fearful also require you to take action and push through the fear. It's much easier to act, to push through the fear, than it is to constantly live with it.

The ABCs of fear are fine and dandy, but until you can clearly recognize your fear you will never break through this giant roadblock. The chart below will help you identify the most common fears faced by students. Once you identify the fear, you can tackle it head on.

TYPES OF FEAR	
FEAR OF FAILURE Sounds like: "I'm not going to waste my time with that stupid business plan competition. I hear the judges are biased anyway."	Translation: "I'm scared to compete in the business plan competition and do poorly."
FEAR OF UNCERTAINTY Sounds like: "I'm not going to move away for college—it would be too expensive."	Translation: "I'm scared of moving to a new city where I don't know anybody."
FEAR OF REJECTION Sounds like: "My boyfriend's under too much pressure with school to tell him about this right now."	Translation: "I'm frightened that if I tell him he'll dump me."
FEAR OF CRITICISM Sounds like: "I don't have time to volunteer for a club."	Translation: "I'm afraid my friends won't think I'm cool if I join a club."
FEAR OF MAKING A POOR DECISION Sounds like: "I'm going to stick with a business degree because it guarantees me the best opportunities."	Translation: "I know drama is my calling but I'm scared that I won't be able to survive as an actor."

SYMPTOMS OF FEAR	
SYMPTOM	EFFECT
Contemplating things too long.	Indecision increases fear. The longer you think about it the more fearful you will become.
SYMPTOM	EFFECT
Finding reasons *why not* instead of *why*.	You will rationalize a reason not to take action and let fear win.
SYMPTOM	EFFECT
Powerless phrases: "I can't," "I have to," "I'll try."	You belittle your control and will not get what you really want .

Now that you know the important facts about fear and how to recognize your own fear, it's time to learn four powerful ways to break through this roadblock so you can take control of your life and feel confident about achieving anything you want.

Four Ways to
FIGHT FEAR

1. Know that you can make the most of any situation
When you are confident in your ability to handle any situation, your fears will no longer limit your actions. This tactic works wonders when it comes to decision-making, such as which direction to steer your career after college.

> LUC:
> A few months before I finished school I was offered a cozy job at a reputable company. It was a great job with a decent salary in a department where I knew almost everyone. Deep down I knew that taking the job wasn't the best thing for me, as entrepreneurship was more my cup of tea. I was terrified

to leave school without a cozy job or a steady paycheck, but I was even more terrified of what my parents would think if I declined the offer. I started to rationalize to myself that starting my own business was too risky, it would require money, it would take time to grow and it might fail. I wallowed in my fear for months. On the day before I had to make my decision I told myself that no matter which decision I made I would be able to handle the outcome—life would go on. I was instantly relieved.

The fear was still there, but knowing I would survive the consequences of either decision gave me the courage to turn down the security of a job and follow my natural inclination to be an entrepreneur—I could handle it. In the beginning, times were tough, money was very tight and success seemed to be a foreign word. However, before long things started to take off, and I experienced opportunity and success beyond my imagination.

You can make the most of whatever you decide—there is no such thing as a best decision. You can't go wrong. To make the most out of any situation, all you need to do is remember these three simple things:

1. You have the ability to handle anything that comes your way.

2. Every challenge contains an invaluable lesson.

3. After your decision is made, let go of your expected outcome and embrace the actual outcome that follows.

   (If you hold onto your expected outcome you will be disappointed by the discrepancy between your expected outcome and the actual outcome, and there is sure to be a difference.)

Reassuring yourself that you can handle the outcome of your decision will help you break through your fear of the unknown, develop confidence, become decisive and feel good about your decision—regardless of what it is.

2. Focus on the benefits

The second tactic to fight fear is to focus on what benefit you will receive once you get past the fear. Remember this: **everything you want in life is on the other side of fear.** This includes success, lasting friendships, a sexy spouse, money, an exciting job, worldly adventures—everything! When you feel fear, visualize the benefit of taking action. For example, if you are fearful to ask for a job, focus on the amazing experience the job will give you. If you are fearful of sitting for your LSAT, MCAT, GMAT, etc., visualize the exciting career opportunities you are creating for yourself. If you are afraid to ask for someone's phone number, focus on the benefit that could result once you get it. The benefits are only possible when you get past the fear, so use the vision of the benefit to propel you into action.

© 1995 TED GOFF

"In this seminar we'll discuss a simple technique for overcoming your fear of speaking in public."

3. Take action

Taking action not only fights fear but it prevents fear from forming and escalating. As Napoleon Hill says in his best-selling book *Think & Grow Rich*, "Indecision crystallizes into doubt, the two blend and become fear!" Skydiving for the first time is a perfect example. As your adventure begins that day, you are filled with excitement for the rush soon to come. Then it becomes time to board the small, toylike plane and venture thousands of feet into the sky. For the next 15 minutes you are stuck on the plane without having the ability to take action and jump. You begin to question the safety of hurling yourself from a moving aircraft with nothing more than a piece of fabric strapped to your back.

> *Feel the fear and do it anyway.*
>
> —Susan Jeffers

When it comes time to jump, your indecision and doubt have escalated into terrifying fear. Your heart begins pounding hard enough to make your shirt wrinkle, and your feet feel permanently cemented to the floor of the plane. Suddenly you jump and the fear is gone! It's just you, thin air, a parachute (one that hopefully works) and an amazing sensation incomparable to anything in this world.

4. See the big picture

When you feel fear creeping up, ask yourself this fear-buster question: "**How does the outcome of this situation affect the rest of my life?**" For example, if you have put off competing in a volleyball tournament because you are scared of doing poorly, and perhaps being criticized by your peers, ask yourself the fear-buster question: "How does the outcome of this volleyball tournament affect the rest of my life?"

You will soon realize that the volleyball tournament is small potatoes in the big scheme of things and that worrying about it is a waste of energy. The same thing can happen when you feel frightened about asking for something, such as help from a professor. This is the fear of rejection—the fear that prevents you from asking. In the big picture of things, the worst that could happen is the prof says no and you don't get help with your assignment. Big deal! Life goes on. No limbs were lost, no blood was shed (assuming you didn't ask for anything offensive!). By seeing the big picture you'll realize that the worst possible outcome is really minor and not worth stressing over. This will give you peace of mind and prevent fear from getting in your way.

> *Death will kill you once, but fear*
> *will kill you over and over*
> *and over again.*
>
> —Marcus Allen

By consistently using these four fear-fighting strategies, you will drastically improve your confidence. How did you feel the very first time you were asked to do a presentation in class? If you are human, you probably had sweaty palms and mumbled your way through it.

After doing many presentations your fear will still be there (remember, it never completely goes away) but your mumbling and sweat stains will have been significantly reduced. Like a good boxer, the more you practice fighting the better you become. The more you practice fighting fear the easier it will be to deliver a knockout punch and stop it from restricting your future. If you become aware of your fears and practice fighting fear, as Joe Rogan says, "Fear is no longer a factor for you."

You can always control procrastination and fear—they are internal roadblocks that you create and can overcome. But what about those situations over which you have no control (snow storms, speeding tickets, full courses, late buses, etc.)? The following are three powerful and proven ways to gain control and get what you want in any situation: be solution-focused, use social reciprocity and ask for what you want.

Be Solution
FOCUSED

Beth Fisher was turning eight years old.
She was eagerly awaiting what was to be her best birthday ever—a party at the Pennsylvania Zoo. Beth loved animals. Her enthusiasm about the event had spread far and wide, resulting in 17 of her family and friends wanting to attend the party. It was going to be a handful but her parents, Peter and Maureen, were willing to do what was necessary to make their daughter's birthday a success. Two years earlier Beth was diagnosed with cystic fibrosis—a genetic disease that drastically reduces one's life span. The Fishers were committed to helping Beth enjoy the fullest life possible, despite the prognosis.

The big day finally arrived and with it, an unwelcome surprise—rain! Not just a drizzle, but a major downpour, forecast to last all day. "Daddy, does this mean we can't go to the zoo today?" Beth asked, her voice concerned. Her father paused, knowing the disappointment she was facing: "I'm afraid so honey, there's not much we can do about Mother Nature—we'll just have to stay indoors, and bring your friends over to the house." His heart ached.

He wished he could do something, but what? As the morning trickled away, Peter suddenly had an idea. If we can't take Beth and her friends to the zoo, why not bring the zoo to them? Quickly he explained his idea to Maureen and in no time the idea was under way. Maureen had a friend who owned a local pet store. The network expanded to include a circus trainer, two clowns and another friend who owned a plant shop. Meanwhile, Beth's grandmother took her shopping for a few hours so everything could be set up without her knowledge. By the time they returned, the basement of Beth's house had been transformed into a safari park! There were lush plants everywhere, and the floor was covered with branches, leaves and rocks. Best of all there were live animals—puppies, kittens, iguanas, and cockatiels—all Beth's favorites. Perched high in the corner was an exotic African parrot, and a little albino pig was intrigued by the two monkeys peering out of a large cage. The party was a massive success, especially since Beth and her friends were anticipating nothing more than chips and Kool-aid. A lion trainer in full uniform was recruited at the last minute and entertained the kids with thrilling jungle stories, while the clowns were busy face-painting all afternoon.

For weeks, Beth's zoo party was the talk of the playground. And even though it took days for the animal aromas to leave the house, the memories would last forever.

Don't let the unexpected rain on your parade, birthday or future plans. Be creative. Seek solutions and stay in control.

Every situation includes the following elements:

1. an objective that you want to accomplish (an unforgettable zoo party with the family)

2. a direct path to reach your objective (trip to the zoo)

3. things out of your control (the weather)

4. things you can control (where you have the zoo experience)

People like Peter Fisher get what they want—an unforgettable zoo party with the family—because they focus on the things they can control. These people think of alternative paths to reach their objectives even when uncontrollable circumstances like bad weather block their direct paths. They are **solution-focused**. People who focus on the things they cannot control give up if the direct route to their objective becomes blocked—they are **blamers**. What about you? Do you give up after the first roadblock, or do you seek alternative solutions?

Successful people seek solutions.
Unsuccessful people seek excuses.

Blamers seldom get what they want because they choose to blame their lack of accomplishment on something else, rather than take the effort to find an alternative route to meet their objective. We all know a few chronic blamers—their favorite words are *if* and *but*:

- "*If* the job market wasn't so bad, I'd be employed by now."

- "*If* I didn't have to work so much I'd be doing much better in school."

- "I would have come to the party, *but* I didn't know the address."

- "I would have studied abroad, *but* they didn't offer all the courses I need."

The more creative you are, the more solutions you will come up with. The more solutions you come up with, the more control you will have over the outcome, and the more likely you will be to achieve your objective.

The Norm of Social RECIPROCITY

Hanna Johanssen was early for class, but her paper wasn't finished.

She approached her professor, who was standing beside the growing stack of due papers. "Dr. Fox, I'm not going to make any excuses. My grandma died 10 times last semester and I have decided to let her rest in peace." Dr. Fox gazed at Hanna, still waiting to hear her creative excuse. "Dr. Fox, my paper isn't finished." Dr. Fox didn't flinch. He continued waiting for the excuse. "In a perfect world I would get an extension until Thursday. However, I understand that the paper is due today and that you set the due date for a specific reason. I don't want to compromise the due date, nor do I want you to put yourself on the line by giving me an extension. This was my own fault and I will live with whatever fate you decide."

Hanna handed Dr. Fox her paper, half the thickness of the others in the submission pile—clearly incomplete—and returned to her seat where she sat attentively for the duration of the class. After class she packed up her belongings and headed towards the door following the herd of students. "Hanna!" called Dr. Fox from the front of the room, "Come here a second." Hanna turned and walked slowly up to the front of the almost-empty classroom. Dr. Fox handed Hanna her paper, "I'll expect to see a complete version of this under my door first thing Thursday morning."

What compelled Dr. Fox to give Hanna an extension? How did she manage to get her way even though she was in the wrong. The answer is called the Norm of Social Reciprocity. This states that it is *normal* for people in *social* situations to *reciprocate*. Basically, this means that when people are given something, they will feel compelled to give something back. Social reciprocity is founded on the distribution of power. In social situations, humans have a natural inclination to keep power balanced at 50:50; they will give or take power until each side has about 50 percent of the control.

Most of us don't realize this and choose to argue profusely when we want something to go our way. However, by arguing we are taking more than 50 percent of the power, causing the other person to argue against us in an effort to regain the power we have taken from them. It's a simple but little-known truth that the best way to gain control of a situation is to first give it up. Sound absurd? It's not. The best way to gain control of a situation is to first give it up. Test it yourself. It sounds weird, but it works!

> When you are arguing with a fool, chances are
> he or she is doing the same.

Hanna put the fate of her assignment in the professor's hands. Dr. Fox felt awkward having all the power. He felt compelled to give something back to Hanna—in this case an extension, which was exactly what she wanted. It is important to note that Hanna didn't give up all the power, however. She kept 10 percent by stating what she wanted—an extension on the paper. It is necessary to keep this 10 percent because it gives the other person, in this case Dr. Fox, a reason to act in your favor.

What would most students have done in Hanna's situation? They likely would have masterminded a grand excuse and fought for their case. "It wasn't my fault," "I didn't receive the e-mail," "My computer crashed"—you've heard them all, probably even used a few at times. This method of making excuses goes completely against the Norm of Social Reciprocity, which is why it is seldom successful. Think about it. With each lie, excuse or argument you are attempting to take power away from your professor. It's no wonder many profs fire back—they want to regain control of the situation. You, Grasshopper, end up with less than what you wanted.

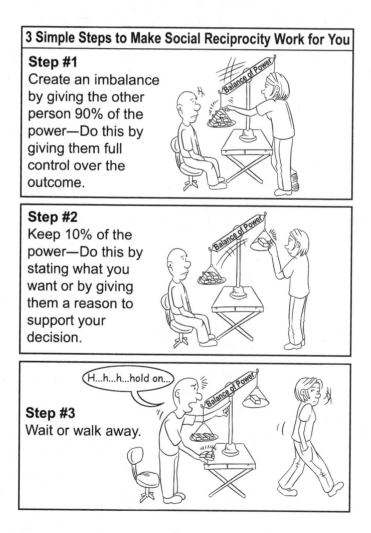

3 Simple Steps to Make Social Reciprocity Work for You

Step #1
Create an imbalance by giving the other person 90% of the power—Do this by giving them full control over the outcome.

Step #2
Keep 10% of the power—Do this by stating what you want or by giving them a reason to support your decision.

Step #3
Wait or walk away.

H...h...h...hold on...

As you are waiting, like Hanna, or walking away, social reciprocity will begin to work its magic. The other person will experience psychological discomfort. This is the awkward sensation that occurs when you shock the other person by giving them full control of the outcome. You have given away so much power, and created such an imbalance, that the other person feels a profound discomfort, compelling him or her to give you something in return.

This happened to Dr. Fox. Psychological discomfort hung over him for the entire class, compelling him to grant Hanna the extension she desired. By granting the extension, the balance of power was restored and Dr. Fox's psychological discomfort was relieved.

> The key to social reciprocity is to create
> psychological discomfort.

To create psychological discomfort, you must genuinely give the other person full control of the outcome. If he or she gets even a faint hint that you are not willing to accept their decision, whatever it may be, psychological discomfort won't be created and you will get a big fat F on your social reciprocity report card.

Why you always win with social reciprocity

Understand that social reciprocity won't work
100 percent of the time, even if you
are completely genuine.

What you *can* be confident about 100 percent
of the time is that you have preserved the
relationship and not burned a
bridge by arguing.

ANDREW:

In my second year at college, modifying cars was the craze—big rims, body kits, turbo chargers—anything to make it look good and go faster. Street racing was a common late-night activity . . . until the police joined the party. To make a long story short, I got pinched racing a buddy of mine. Knowing that the fine would lead to a suspension of my license and double my already exorbitant insurance, I did what I thought I had to do—I lied. I told the cop that he was mistaken and that it wasn't me racing. "Must have been another black sports car," I blurted in an obviously nervous tone. He looked at me with pity, told me to stay put and went to talk to my friend in the other car.

My friend figured I had come clean and proceeded to cooperate with the cop, accepting the consequences of racing. After a short discussion my friend drove off—no ticket, no argument, nothing! Just as the cop was returning to my vehicle, I was alerted by a well-timed text message from my friend. It read: **TELL THE TRUTH.** I quickly adjusted my strategy. "Officer," I stammered, "I lied to you. I was racing and deserve the ticket. I should not have lied, but I'm a student and losing my license would make things very tough." I was being sincere and he could tell.

"I know you are just doing your job and I'll just have to live with your decision." The cop looked at me with a long, hard stare. I had just granted him power over my fate and he knew it. After what seemed like an hour, he returned with a pink ticket in hand. On the top of the ticket was my new favorite word: *warning*. It was just a warning! Thank God. Driving to school that semester never felt so good.

In this scenario (after the well-timed text message) 90 percent of the control was handed over to the officer and 10 percent was kept by simply stating, "I'm a student and losing my license would make things tough." The police officer could not handle the psychological discomfort of being granted the majority of the power and naturally reciprocated by giving something in return—a much-appreciated warning.

The cop story and Hanna's story are clear examples of how social reciprocity works wonders when you are in the wrong. This is when social reciprocity works best. However, social reciprocity can also be used in day-to-day situations. When you want to watch your choice of movie, for example, if your friend asks what movie do you want to see, what is your natural response? Do you firmly attest that you want to see the new action thriller? Or do you briefly mention your movie of choice and proceed to let your friend make the final decision? If you do the latter and say something like, "I hear the new action thriller is great, but I don't care, you choose," you have given your friend power over the movie selection, and created psychological discomfort. There is a good probability that your friend will reciprocate, and more often than not your evening will be spent watching the action thriller.

Using social reciprocity will give you control of situations you once thought were hopeless. What is more eye-opening is realizing the consequences of not using this tool. The following story, as told by Dr. Jerry Gray of the I.H. Asper School of Business, shows what can happen if you do not use social reciprocity in your day-to-day interactions and unknowingly take power away from others.

Charlie McDaid used to work for a major airline in Montreal.

At the start of a busy Saturday one of the employees called in sick. When short of staff, the airline's policy was to eliminate the first-class line and have just a single line for everyone. Charlie felt bad about doing this because it created a very long line-up, but he knew that the plane would still leave on time and it was his only option. An obviously wealthy couple draped in luxurious furs and reeking of arrogance barged up to the front of the line throwing their first-class tickets at Charlie. "You people are treating us like cattle," the man exclaimed. "We flew with the Secretary of State last week and we never wait in lines!"

The man was wearing so much gold he could hardly stand up—more chains than brains, as some would say. Charlie tried diplomatically to get the man to calm down, but the more he tried the more vicious the guy became. The man cursed the airline and even personally attacked Charlie, shouting, "You're as incompetent as the airline you work for!" Charlie finally gave the couple their boarding passes and they took a seat to wait for their boarding call.

The rich man and his wife were on their way to Glasgow and the man had checked his golf clubs. As Charlie was about to put the golf clubs on the baggage carousel he stopped, looked around to see that no one was watching, then reached down and took off the tag that said Glasgow and replaced it with one for Hong Kong. "The biggest disappointment of my career is that I couldn't have been in the Glasgow airport when that moron found out his golf clubs went to Hong Kong," exclaimed Charlie. "I felt childish, I felt immature, I felt like a kid, but I had to somehow get that guy back."

The rich man is going to think the whole thing was an accident, when really it was social reciprocity backfiring on him. The rich man felt he could control the situation by arguing. However, what he had done was make Charlie feel powerless, compelling Charlie to take power back and even the score.

> If you take power away from someone,
> they will find a way to take some back.

Do you try and control situations by arguing, proving the facts to get your way? Has your luggage ever been lost?

Social reciprocity works because 98.75 percent of people on earth want to help you out. People take no inherent glee in watching you get screwed (unless you take all their power away). You don't hear people say, "I had a great day. I screwed 10 people today!" People want to help, even when you are in the wrong. So, whether you are in the wrong or not, give others 90 percent of the power to decide your fate. The outcome will be far more favorable than if you push to gain control by arguing.

The Power of ASKING

Have you ever felt frustrated because you got lost driving? Your appointment starts in five minutes, and you have no idea where the building is. You were told to turn right at the second set of lights, and you did—now you're lost. How do you end up where you wanted to be? Chances are good that the sooner you asked someone the sooner you got to your appointment.

Asking is the third powerful and proven way to increase your control in any situation. By asking you increase your knowledge, and by using this knowledge you gain control over the situation and increase the likelihood of getting what you want —whether it be directions to an appointment or instructions on what to study for an upcoming exam.

How can college cost so much?

New Jersey high school students Chris Barrett and Luke McCabe were shocked to discover that one year at a private university could cost up to $40,000. An idea hit them while they were watching golf on TV. "We saw a commercial with Tiger Woods wearing a Nike hat and we thought, if Tiger Woods can get all this money being sponsored, why can't we?" said Chris.

Chris and Luke decided they were going to be the first corporately sponsored college students by becoming "spokesguys" for a wholesome company—tobacco and alcohol excluded.

They set up a unique website, www.chrisandluke.com, complete with pictures of the pair wearing t-shirts that stated, "Your logo goes here," and hats saying, "www.YourSite.com." Chris and Luke ended up with 20 companies who were interested in becoming sponsors for their college tuition. In the end they chose First USA, one of the nation's largest credit card companies.

Within 48 hours of the first national announcement they garnered over 12 million dollars in publicity and over 80 million media impressions. Overnight these two "sponsored" students became the talk of America—being featured on *The Today Show*, ABC, NBC, FOX, CNN, in *People* magazine, the *New York Times* and on over 400 radio shows.

It all started with an idea and having the courage to ask.

Chris and Luke went from being two typical kids to sponsored college all-stars being featured in major motion pictures. Not to mention they had their tuition costs paid for. This was achieved solely because they asked, then asked some more, then asked some more. The world responds to those who ask, just as it did for Chris and Luke. Are you feeling stuck, not moving closer to what you really want? If this is the case, you probably aren't doing enough asking.

> *Insanity: doing the same thing over and over again and expecting different results.*
>
> —Albert Einstein

As we stated earlier, 98.75 percent of all people want to help you. That means that 98 times out of a 100 (or 9,875 times out of 10,000 to be exact) people will respond to you in a way that is helpful—that's a lot better odds than winning the lottery or finding a $20 bill in your couch, so what are you waiting for?

Good things to ask for . . .

1. help on an assignment
2. advice on courses to take
3. discounts (use your student status to your advantage)
4. advice on extracurricular activities to get involved in
5. clarification on confusing concepts presented in class
6. contact information of people you want to stay in touch with

---

The odds are in your favor that people will help you . . . but you must ask.

Why Not ASK?

Asking is something that doesn't come naturally to most people. That's okay, because it's like riding a bike—with a little practice you'll soon get the hang of it. Let's look at the three most common barriers that stop people from asking.

1. It's rude to ask

Some people are told—by society, by parents, by someone —that it is rude to ask for what you want. The reason for this message likely stems from fear, or is passed on from the generation before as blindly as it was passed on to you. Regardless of where it came from, this school of thought is false. It's perfectly acceptable to ask for what you want, and until you believe this, asking will be very difficult. If asking is rude, wouldn't more guys get smacked upside the head after proposing to their girlfriends?

2. Lack of confidence

When asking, most people stumble over their words and end up muttering something much less than they really wanted, if they ask at all. This is due to a lack of confidence. A confident request has a much greater chance of receiving a positive response. If you do not prepare to ask with confidence, you are sabotaging your chances of getting what you want even before you ask.

3. Fear of rejection

Asking for less than you want (or not asking at all) happens for one major reason—FEAR OF REJECTION. Don't be scared to ask for a phone number, directions to an appointment or an extension on an assignment. The worst they can say is *no*, and rest assured, the big N-O will not kill you. If you ask and someone says no, you will be exactly where you started—you have nothing to lose, so ask!

How to ask

To ask effectively you must:

1. know specifically what you want
2. believe it is possible to get it
3. ask clearly

The next time you go to ask for something, refer back to these three things. Asking effectively will greatly improve your chances of getting what you want.

Asking can make you feel awkward and uncomfortable. This is natural. Give yourself permission to feel awkward so the discomfort won't hold you back.

Remember, **you will only get what you ask for, so ask for what you want!**

CONCLUSION

With the tools from this chapter in your toolbox, you have everything you need to reach your goals.

Roadblock #1—Procrastination

Procrastination prevents you from reaching your goals, causing regret and "if only's." There are four ways to fight procrastination:

1. Become Mechanical—turn dreaded tasks into painless routines.
2. The Sausage Method—break large, daunting tasks into smaller components.
3. Your To-Do-Today list—your important tasks for the day in priority order.
4. Find your *why*—visualize a strong reason why you should take action.

Roadblock #2—Fear

The ABCs of fear—A, fear does not go away; B, it stems from uncertainty; C, it's easier to push through it than live with it.
Four Ways to Fight Fear:

1. Know that you can make the most of ANY situation.
2. Focus on the benefits of pushing through fear.
3. Take action.
4. Ask, "How does the outcome affect the rest of my life?"

How to Get What You Want in Any Situation

Be Solution-focused
- Focus on finding solutions and you will increase your control over the outcome.

Social Reciprocity
- If you want to get your way, give the other person the power over the outcome. They will feel inclined to give you something in return.
- No one wins an argument.

Asking
- You only get what you ask for, so ask for what you want.

> It's time to shatter those roadblocks. To accelerate to what you really want, don't miss the Action Steps that follow.

ACTION STEPS

Online version available in *The Focus Zone* at:
www.focusedstudent.com

Fight Procrastination

Flex Your Fear Muscle

Can You Get What You Want?

Fight Procrastination

What two things do you procrastinate about the most? (Examples: studying, writing papers, working out, cleaning your bedroom.)

1. _____

2. _____

For each of the things you procrastinate about above, select a fighting method—become mechanical, sausage method, to-do-today list, finding your reason why—that you will use to break through each of these procrastination roadblocks.

On the following page, describe how you will specifically use this method in the next two weeks to overcome this procrastination and feel good about your accomplishment. (Example: I will use the sausage method to study for my chemistry exam productively. I will study one chapter of chemistry every day this week and review my notes on the day before the exam.)

1. _____

_____

_____

2. _____

_____

_____

Flex Your Fear Muscle

Do something daring and a little risky every week—talk to a stranger in your class, volunteer to make a presentation, ask that cute guy or girl out on a date. This habit will keep your life exciting, make you more confident and allow you to push through fear with ease.

List two things you can do in the next seven days that will flex your fear muscle and help you become accustomed to taking risks. (Examples: ask three questions in geology class, ask David to the dance, sign up for intramural basketball.) Feel like a risk taker? Check out *The Focus Zone* at www.focusedstudent.com for cool "risky" ideas.

1. _____

_____

2. _____

_____

Can You Get What You Want?

Describe a current roadblock you are faced with that is preventing you from getting what you want. (Examples: increasing your grade on an assignment, drop date has passed for a class you want to switch out of.)

What method will work best to help you get around the roadblock so you can get what you want?

a)   Be solution-focused

b)   Social reciprocity

c)   Asking for what you want

_____

_____

How will you use this method to ensure you get what you want?

_____

_____

_____

_____

One day I will get help with my
procrastination problem.

—Anonymous

It Ain't WHAT You Know, It's WHO You Know

*Eighty percent of life's satisfaction
comes from meaningful relationships.*

—Brian Tracy

Erin Arenshaw had it all figured out.
As long as she attended a reputable college and pulled off really good grades, the job of her dreams was bound to materialize. Her parents and teachers had emphasized the importance of top marks all the way through junior and senior high school. Erin had stayed true to this advice and was determined to maintain her status as a high achiever throughout college.

She was accepted to one of the best colleges in the east and before long she was neck deep in assignments, group projects and unfathomable amounts of reading. Erin's part-time modeling job was quick to vanish from her schedule and so too were coffee dates with friends, morning runs and volunteering for the student newspaper. She kept her priorities in order, doing what was needed to stay on track with her goal.

Erin's strategy worked. She graduated as class valedictorian with a near-perfect GPA. She could hardly wait to sort through the mountain of job offers that would soon be coming her way. But as the end of her final semester approached, a curious thing happened. Erin's friends, the ones she had put to the side during her studies, were finding interesting jobs with excellent starting salaries. They had degrees, too, but they were never in a serious relationship with their textbooks the way Erin had been. Erin was mystified. Why were they landing the great jobs instead of her?

A few months later Erin's mother had the entire family over for dinner. The dreaded question poked itself into the conversation. "So Erin, where are you working these days?" asked her uncle. After dinner Erin went on to tell him about her frustrations. Her uncle responded, "Erin, think about it like this: there are thousands of actors in Hollywood. All of them can memorize the same lines, much like how you memorized your textbooks. The actors who get the auditions, and subsequently the part, are the ones who know people in the industry."

Her uncle did some calling around and arranged a meeting with his friend Mike Costache, the chairman of the Young Professionals Global Network (*www.ypgn.org*). Her uncle also had a contact at Monitor, a Boston-based consulting firm. Within two weeks, Erin had interviewed at three companies and had her choice of attractive jobs.

For Erin, this was a huge wake-up call. She found out the hard way that good grades alone didn't guarantee a dream job. Her uncle had provided the missing link—it's *who* you know, and who others know, that opens the door to opportunity. Erin had finally been introduced to the art of networking.

Sadly, it is rare to find a course in college that teaches us how to build relationships. The focus is on *what* you know, rather than *who* you know. This drastically limits your opportunities as a student. Overwhelmingly, it is who we know that will get us places in life—especially when it comes to finding a job. Don't expect to learn this in a college course, but do expect the college environment to provide dozens of opportunities to build lasting personal and professional relationships. By reading this chapter and completing the Action Steps, you will learn powerful and crucial skills not taught in school—how to build excellent relationships, how to make exciting new contacts and how to continually add value to other people so that everything you need is just a phone call away.

Eight Ways to be Liked
BY EVERYONE

Who enjoys being admired, respected and liked? We all do! Why do you think ridiculous pranks, nicknames and drunken stupidity are rampant during freshman year? The answer is simple: people want to fit in, be cool and be liked. Unfortunately, these are examples of attention-seeking activities that don't foster long-term relationships. The foundation of building relationships lies in knowing how to treat people so they genuinely like you. If people like you they will stay in touch with you, find ways to add value to your life and always be willing to help. The following timeless principles have been tested and taught for centuries. They are simple truths that have been researched, written about and applied by some of the most famous authors, teachers and leaders of our time—Dale Carnegie, Charles Schwab and John D. Rockefeller included. When you apply these eight principles to your life, you'll be more likable and have a wide range of friends.

1. Make the other person feel important
Imagine the following scenario: you are chatting with a recent graduate at a career information night. In conversation you casually ask, "What did you major in?" Expecting nothing more than a one- or two-word reply, instead what you get is the following 16-word tongue-twister: "Bachelor of neurological science and molecular genetics honors with a biochemical minor and the co-op option," they respond with pride.

To you this might sound like gibberish, but to the owner of that degree it is music to their ears. You may not realize it, but this is a golden opportunity to make a friend. What would be a good response to the tongue twister? The following quote will give you a hint.

> *The deepest urge in human nature is*
> *the desire to be important.*
>
> —Dr. John Dewey

Admiring the 16-word degree title will make you a friend much faster than shrugging it off as a goofy degree title. You have been given a sneak peek into what makes the other person feel important. Whether it is admiring a fancy title or acknowledging someone's contribution on a project, the act of making others feel important will build lasting friendships and leave you adored by anyone you meet. This concept is the core of building relationships. Feeling important quenches the thirst of our ego like water does for our bodies. Anyone will like you if you make that person feel important, and do so sincerely.

Write it down—**the deepest urge in human nature is to feel important.** Make others feel important and they will like you forever.

2. What is it like in their shoes?

Next time someone cuts you off on the freeway, before you tell him to remove his head from another part of his body, ask yourself this:

- "Why is that person driving like a maniac?"

- "I wonder what it would be like to stand in his shoes right now?"

- "What is causing this person to be so reckless?"

For all you know, the driver of that car might be a father who is rushing to the hospital where his five-year-old daughter is critically injured.

Rage Reduction

When someone does something that frustrates us, it triggers an automatic anger response (the middle finger, four-letter words, flying karate kicks). To counteract this tendency, in the split second before this anger kicks in, STOP and force yourself to ask this magic question:

"Isn't that interesting?"

When you do this, you interrupt your natural anger response. Pausing to ask this question will help you understand where the other person is coming from. You also prevent yourself from reacting in a way you may later regret. Isn't that interesting?

When you are frustrated at a group member, annoyed at your parents, upset at a friend or cut off by a careless driver, first seek to understand that person's behavior before reacting to it. By taking a moment to understand the other person's feelings, you will prevent arguments, save friendships, avoid unneeded stress and ultimately build stronger relationships.

3. Shut your big mouth

Have you ever been listening to someone, or pretending to listen, when really all you were doing was waiting for them to finish so you could start talking? Most people do this. Why? Because we feel important when we share our experiences and opinions with others. That, however, is precisely why it is so important to shut your big mouth and let the other person do most of the talking. If you allow others to speak about themselves, and if you take genuine interest in what they are saying, they will talk at length and adore you for letting them.

4. Appreciate what people do

A simple and sincere "thank you" is a powerful yet highly ignored tool for building relationships. By demonstrating that you appreciate what someone has done for you, you'll stand out from the crowd and be remembered and respected. Think about the last time someone sincerely thanked you. How did it make you feel? What were your feelings toward the person who thanked you? If you are like most people, you really appreciated the thank you and highly respect the person who said it.

According to Hallmark, 58 percent of moms say their kids write thank-you notes. Did you write thank-you notes when you were a kid? Do you write them now? Only three percent of adults (yes, that includes students) still send thank-you cards—a big decrease since kindergarten.

Don't let age be the factor that prevents you from saying thank you. Make a habit of giving compliments and expressing your gratitude (especially when it is least expected). This will not only make others like you, but you'll brighten their day and feel good about doing so.

5. Know thy name

Visualize this all-too-familiar scenario: you and a friend are walking down the hall when all of a sudden you are brought to a halt. Your friend Jacelynn has run into her friends Randy and Rebecca and a conversation has erupted. Meanwhile, you are standing aimlessly off to one side, counting staples on the wall. To reduce the awkwardness, Jacelynn pulls you into the group and introduces you. The conversation ends. "It was nice meeting you, Jane," say Randy and Rebecca as they turn to leave. You begin to reply, but oh, no! You've already forgotten their names! A moment of awkward silence follows. "Uh, nice meeting you too," you manage to blurt out, before scurrying away down the hall. A week later you're walking down the same hall and sure enough, your two new mystery acquaintances are just steps away. You know they see you, and they know you've seen them, but you just look at the ground, hoping you can sneak by without saying a word.

A person's name is to that person the
sweetest and most important sound
in any language.

—Dale Carnegie

When you forget someone's name or, worse, call someone by the wrong name, your self-confidence is eroded. The potential of building a relationship with this person is severely reduced. Remembering people's names keeps your confidence intact. Consider making Randy and Rebecca new friends instead of the couple you purposely avoid whenever they get within 10 feet. The exception, of course, is when someone is incredibly annoying—in that case staring at the ground is a great avoidance strategy.

You have come to Treasure #6. If you don't have a photographic memory, you might be interested in learning two flawless and simple methods for remembering people's names. Go to *The Focus Zone* at *www.focusedstudent.com* to collect your treasure and prevent the embarrassment from ever muttering the wrong name again!

6. Smile

Imagine the following scenario: it has been a long day at school —you're exhausted, stressed out and dreading the big exam you have the next morning. As you enter your home, a big, hairy, tail-wagging friend anxiously greets you with an enthusiastic grin. You switch to your doggie voice and you drop to your knees to share a moment with your furry friend. How do you feel now? Probably much better than before you walked through the door. What is it about a dog's warm greeting that fills us with joy? Consider this a dog's lesson: if you want people to like you and feel energized in your presence, then smile often and greet people with enthusiasm.

The bottom line is: people like people who smile. Smiles are contagious, and they are the ultimate energy booster. How many times in a day do you smile? Could you be smiling more?

7. Do what you say

This is big stuff—there is no such thing as an insignificant promise. Once you say, "I'll call you later . . .," "I'll be there at noon . . .," "I'll e-mail you the information . . .," "I'll clean the bathroom . . .," "I'll send you my resume. . .," you have entered into an agreement with someone. One of two things will happen:

1. You do what you said you would, increasing the trust the other person has in you.

2. You don't follow through on your promise, causing the person to lose trust in you.

Once you have broken your word a few times, you will be labeled unreliable, not to be trusted. Unreliable people cause frustration, and this frustration eventually leads to broken relationships. People like people who they can count on.

> Every broken relationship stems from
> a broken agreement.

Can you be counted on? Do you always keep your word? If you always do what you say, you'll build trust in your relationships. If you keep breaking agreements, you'll rupture relationships. It's better to be known as a reliable straight shooter than a flake!

8. Give more than you take

Stephen Covey, renowned author of *The 7 Habits of Highly Effective People,* makes the analogy of relationships being like bank accounts—you make deposits and withdrawals. The more deposits you make, the more money you have available for withdrawal. If you continue taking withdrawals without making deposits, your bank account will soon go into arrears. Relationships work the same way.

Are you the one always asking for a ride? Money? Attention? Forgiveness? If you keep taking more than you give in your relationships, you'll erode them until nothing is left—losing friends one withdrawal at a time. If you want to have rich relationships, then make it a habit to add value to others—make deposits to these relationships—so you have a pool of people willing to help when you need it most.

If you follow the eight principles above, you will notice a significant improvement in the way people treat you. Don't be surprised when your phone begins to ring more often.

Next, we will show you how to build a network of influential contacts that will take you backstage—beyond your classroom walls, beyond resumes and high grades and into a world of opportunity where promising futures are born.

In Sports it's a Team, in Life
IT'S A NETWORK

Life is a team sport. Everyone has a team of supporters helping every step of the way. The doctor cut your umbilical cord when you were two minutes old, your parents tied your shoes until you were four and your bus driver drove you to school until you were old enough to drive. As you grow older the need for a team doesn't fade away; in fact, the need grows and the team evolves.

The world is an *interdependent* place where everyone is *inter*connected and *dependent* on each other. Confusion often arises between what is meant by INdependent and INTER-dependent. We know the spelling is similar and it's hard on the eyes, so let's begin by defining these terms.

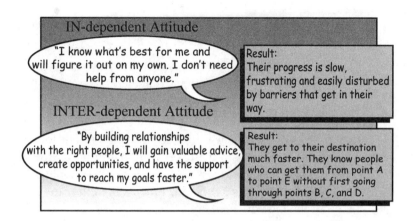

People who have an interdependent attitude build relationships through networking. You've probably heard the buzzwords network or networking. If not, consider this an introduction:

Network:
The web of people you know that you add value to, or who can add value to you.

Networking:
The unstructured process of building mutually rewarding relationships with others.

What Networking is Not!

Networking has a bad rep on the street. Some people think "networking" is an activity for business students only, not for all students OR (even worse) they perceive networking as building relationships with people so they can be USED and ABUSED at a later date when they need them.

This is not true. A network is made of relationships that are give and take, and networking is for all students, because in any discipline it ain't WHAT you know, it's WHO you know that will help you get where you want in life—you need a network.

Here are some startling facts about the importance of a network:

- 80 percent of jobs are never posted to the public, but are filled through referrals and contacts.

- One job is offered for every 1,470 resumes submitted.

- Rich Bolles, the nations leading job hunt expert, has found that applying online and using resumes have only a 4 to 7 percent success rate whereas asking family and people you know (your network) is four times more likely to land you the job you want.

Are you interdependent, using your network? Or are you independent, trying to do it all on your own? A network is a powerful tool and can open doors that would be impossible to open on your own.

No matter how smart you are, no matter
how talented, you can't do it alone.

—Harvey MacKay

The following excerpt from the #1 *New York Times* best-seller *The Tipping Point* proves how any door you need opened is within your reach, or better said, within the reach of a few people you know.

In the late 1960s, the psychologist Stanley Milgram conducted an experiment to find an answer to what is known as the small-world problem. The problem is this: how are human beings connected? Do we all belong to separate worlds, operating simultaneously but auto-nomously, so that the links between any two people, anywhere in the world are few and distant? Or are we all bound up together in a grand, interlocking web?

Milgram's idea was to test this question with a chain letter. He got the names of 160 people who lived in Omaha, Nebraska, and mailed each of them a packet. In the packet was the name and address of a stockbroker who worked in Boston and lived in Sharon, Massachusetts. Each person was instructed to write his or her name on the packet and send it on to a friend or acquaintance who he or she thought would get the packet closer to the stockbroker. For example, if you lived in Omaha and had a cousin outside of Boston, you might send it to him, on the grounds that—even if your cousin did not himself know the stockbroker— he would be a lot more likely to be able to get to the stockbroker in two or three or four steps. The idea was that when the packet finally arrived at the stockbroker's house, Milgram could look at the list of all those whose hands it went through to get there and establish how closely connected someone chosen at random from one part of the country was to another person in another part of the country. Milgram found that most of the letters reached the stockbroker in five or six steps.

This experiment and similar ones performed by Stanley Milgram gave birth to the popular phenomenon called "six degrees of separation." Six degrees of separation is the theory that anyone on the planet can be connected to any other person on the planet through a chain of acquaintances that has no more than five intermediaries. What does this mean for you? It means by default, you are at most six people away from anyone you want to contact. By growing your network, your degrees of separation decrease. It doesn't take long before anyone you want to contact, pitch an idea to or work for is only a couple of phone calls away. Think about your possibilities. The system you are about to learn will show you how to build a solid network and add anybody to it.

The Three-Step, Sure-Fire
NETWORKING SYSTEM

When you grow a flower, you must start with a seed, then you must plant the seed in a location where it can grow, and finally you must nurture the budding flower by providing it with water and sunlight. Networking is no different. Growing and maintaining a network is like caring for a flower. You need initial contact and ongoing nurturing for your network to grow. Here is a three-step, sure-fire system to grow and maintain a powerful network.

1. Make the contact

By using the eight ways to be liked by everyone, you'll be able to kick-start a relationship with anyone you meet.

So you meet someone—now what? Before that person can enter your network, he or she needs to pass a quality inspection. If you skip the quality inspection, you'll end up diluting your good contacts with not-so-good contacts. Being a busy student, the time you have to build relationships is limited so you want to build the best relationships possible with the best people. You are doing a disservice to yourself and to the other person if you cannot add value to them or they cannot add value to you. We like the three quality-inspection questions that networking guru Harvey Mackay uses before adding someone to his network:

1. Are they adding me to their network?
2. Was the meeting memorable, enjoyable and worth repeating?
3. Do they know something or someone I want to know?

If the answers to these three questions are yes, yes, yes, the person passes the quality inspection—your network's bouncer—making him or her ready for the next stage.

Before you can effectively move to the next stage, you must first complete a small but critically important task—capturing information. The easiest way to do this is to scribble a few notes on the back of the other person's business card (be sure to ask for one!). Here's an example of important info to include:

If the person doesn't have a business card (students often do not), then a scrap piece of paper or even a used napkin will do the trick. The important thing is that you capture as much information as possible and do it quickly.

> Want to show someone you care?
> Demonstrate you remember.

When is a pot of coffee the freshest? After it has sat for three hours? No. Same with information in your brain—it's fresh immediately after you make contact. The longer you wait to write it down, the more information you forget and the colder the relationship becomes. If you don't have good, well-documented information, it will be much harder to complete the next two steps.

ANDREW:
After I had attended a few student conferences, a collection of business cards began forming in my bedroom. I had scribbled notes on the back of most of them, but my hideous chicken-scratch writing was barely legible and the space was limited. My friend David showed me a fantastic system that works wonders if you use a Palm Pilot or other brand of PDA. After meeting someone David wanted to add to his network, he would input their contact information into his Palm Pilot then open a "note" in the same address file (you can do this on practically any PDA). In this note section he would write key information about the person—the same topics outlined on the business card on the previous page. As the months rolled on, David was diligent about keeping these notes updated—adding new information whenever it came in. Birthdays, favorite sports teams, upcoming holidays . . . whatever he wanted to remember.

By simply referring to these notes, David always knew where people were working, what their interests were and how he could help them. As well, if he ever needed something he could go into his digital address list (his network) and find the perfect person to ask. I caught onto this brilliant system during my junior year. By the time I graduated I had over a thousand people digitally crammed into my Palm Pilot, including friends from across the world, business owners, national recruiters, millionaires and even a few celebrities. Sadly, I also acquired the nickname "Palm Pilot" among my roommates. Having a note attached to many of these people's address files allows me to remember the little details that I would otherwise forget. It still astounds me how well this simple system works.

2. Follow-up

Follow-up is the difference between meeting someone and networking. Chatting up a cutie or a hunk at a party is meeting someone. Getting their phone number and calling them the next day is networking (or, in this case, picking up). When you follow up with someone you have met, you are demonstrating that you value the person and want to form a relationship. Common ways of following up include a brief phone call, a thank-you card or an e-mail.

When following up, remember these four important items:

1. where you met and what you talked about (just in case the person doesn't remember your name)

2. a thank you to show that you got value from meeting them

3. a "go-forward." This is the next possible step for keeping in touch—information you will send, a referral to someone, a meeting for coffee, etc. If there is no apparent go-forward, use a generic statement like, "I look forward to keeping in touch."

4. your contact info—networking is about who knows you as much as it is about who you know

Once you have followed up, the person is halfway in the door of your network. The next step will ensure he or she enters.

3. Adding value

So you met Greg at a billiards night held by a club you are associated with. You recall Greg saying he loves race cars. A few weeks later you are flipping through *TIME* magazine and notice a great article on race cars. What do you do? You e-mail Greg to let him know, or better yet, mail him the magazine with a little note that says, "I thought you might enjoy this . . ." Do you think Greg will be willing to help you next time you need something? Of course! You have added value to this contact.

Dig your well before you're thirsty.

—Harvey MacKay

Say you met a recruiter of an accounting firm at a career fair. A few months later you are on a committee, planning a conference that many senior accounting students will be attending. What do you do? You tell the recruiter about the event and send her a VIP invitation. She will be very impressed by your thought and get a lot of value from being able to attend and scope out the new batch of accounting grads. When it comes time to find a job, do you think this recruiter will give you preference over another accounting student? Of course! You have added value to this contact.

LUC:
I had only two weeks remaining on my study abroad in London, England. It was a typical Saturday night and I had gone out with some friends. On the walk home as I got to my street I saw a flood of police cruisers and fire engines. I walked eagerly down the sidewalk, my eyes wide open, trying to figure out what all the excitement was about. That was when it dawned on me. The center of everyone's attention was my house . . . or the lack of it. I will never forget the feeling in my stomach when I looked up at my bedroom window and could see nothing more than a black hole. My house had caught fire. Only the brick foundation remained.

My pictures, my passport, my computer, my clothes, my books . . . EVERYTHING was gone. Everything I owned had been in that house. The knot in my stomach only grew tighter. There I was, in a foreign country with nothing but the shirt on my back—literally. I slowly reached into my pocket and pulled out my cell phone. Even though my material possessions were destroyed, I still had what mattered most—a network of great people, friends and family who I could count on. I started dialing. It was time to test the strength of my network and take a drink from the well.

When you add value to someone, he or she becomes part of your network

Add value to your network on a consistent basis so that your network "well" will have plenty of water in it when you need a drink. Even if you meet a Fortune 500 CEO, a star basketball player or a billionaire, you can add value to that person and make him or her part of your network. You can add value to anyone, which means you can add anyone to your network. Let us repeat this important point—**you can add value to anyone, which means you can add anyone to your network.**

Four Ways to Add Value to Others

SEND THEM INFORMATION

Send them an article, a picture from the event you met them at, an inspiring quote or any other information they will value. If you know their interests and hobbies, it will be easy to find information they will appreciate.

DO WHAT YOU SAY

Following through with any promises you make to people when you meet them will quickly gain their respect.

ASK THEM HOW YOU CAN ASSIST

The simple question "So what can I do for you?" will open up the door to dozens of ways you can add value to that contact.

SHARE A CONTACT

You may not be able to assist them or add value directly, but you probably know someone else who can—make the connection.

Your Networking
NEIGHBORHOOD

Your networking neighborhood is comprised of all the great places you can meet potential candidates to add to your network. Your neighborhood is important, because it kick-starts the entire networking process. The following diagram breaks the networking neighborhood into three places: social, professional and other.

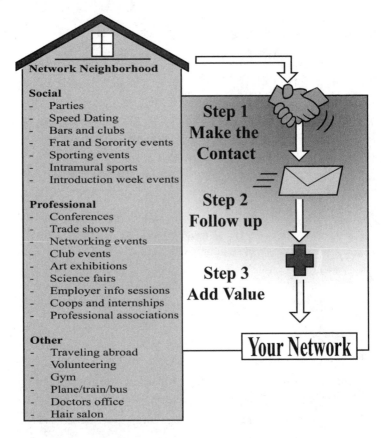

Network Neighborhood

Social
- Parties
- Speed Dating
- Bars and clubs
- Frat and Sorority events
- Sporting events
- Intramural sports
- Introduction week events

Professional
- Conferences
- Trade shows
- Networking events
- Club events
- Art exhibitions
- Science fairs
- Employer info sessions
- Coops and internships
- Professional associations

Other
- Traveling abroad
- Volunteering
- Gym
- Plane/train/bus
- Doctors office
- Hair salon

Step 1
Make the
Contact

Step 2
Follow up

Step 3
Add Value

Your Network

After you meet someone in your network neighborhood, you can take them through the easy three-step, sure-fire networking system: making the contact, following up and adding value. This is the full meal-deal—how you can build any size of network you want that can help you with anything you desire. It is not where you meet someone that counts; it is making the effort to meet the person that is important. If your opportunities in life depend on *who* you know and not *what* you know, then what are you willing to do to build the *who*?

80/20 rule of networking

The more time you spend in your network neighborhood the more people you will be able to add to your network (which is a good thing). However, as your network grows it will become harder to stay in touch and add value to everyone—time is limited. An Italian economist found the answer to this pressing dilemma. Over 100 years ago, Vilfredo Pareto came to the realization that 80 percent of the wealth in Italy was held by 20 percent of the population.

After explaining this phenomenon to his friends in the fields of astronomy, mathematics, chemistry and physics, it became obvious that the 80/20 rule could be applied to their fields as well. Your network is no exception to this timeless rule —80 percent of the value, the love, the attention, the favors, and the Christmas cards come from 20 percent of the people in your network.

LUC:
I call the top people in my network my "star list" and I put a * beside their names in my address book. These people make up around 20 percent of my network, but they give me at least 80 percent of the value, if not 90 percent. I make sure I don't miss the birthdays of my star contacts, and I spend a lot of my time ensuring I add value to them on a continual basis. The only challenge I've had with my

system is when people ask me, "Why do some names have stars beside them, and why don't I have one?" I haven't found a good response to that one yet.

Who deserves a star in your address book? The answer is people who have big networks themselves, people who you get along with and people who share similar interests. It can also include people who are heading in the same direction as you, people who you admire and can learn from, people who continually add value to your life and people who you take pride in assisting. It's important to know who these people are so you can focus your energy where it adds the most contribution to those relationships. If you don't, the relationship you have with these star contacts will weaken rather than flourish.

You Are Who You HANG WITH

Although we went to different colleges, we both experienced a similar challenge with many of our high school friends. When we first arrived at college there were dozens of opportunities to make new friends. In no time we had a new crew of people to party and study with. We stayed in touch with our high school friends back home and they even came to visit on a few occasions.

In our second year we started to notice a difference between ourselves and some of these old friends back home. They were saying the same jokes, hanging at the same places and talking about past events—nothing had changed. The first few trips home were exciting because we got to relive the old times. After a few more trips, however, it started to become a drag hanging out with some of these people—they were heading in a different direction and had different ambitions (some had a total lack of ambition). As time passed, it occurred to us that they were not growing, and unless we wanted to slow our own growth we had to jump ship.

It was an EXTREMELY difficult realization. We had to let go of some of our most cherished friends from the glory days of high school because maintaining the relationships had become a burden. The process of letting go of a few of these friends was difficult, and it continued to be throughout college and even after college, as more and more relationships were concluded. Letting go did not mean breaking the relationship or never talking to the person again. It simply meant choosing to spend time with different people.

We will always care about these old friends and always say hello when given the opportunity, but they have stopped adding value to our lives, and the value we can add to them is limited. Since this realization, we have been able to focus our time on building relationships with like-minded friends who support our ideas, share our ambitions and can relate to our college experiences. This has allowed us to accelerate forward rather than being stuck in the past.

A note of caution is necessary here. As it was for us, it may be difficult for you to identify who these people are, and it is going to be even more difficult to let go of these relationships. However, to continue moving forward it must be done. The truth is that neither you nor the other person is getting much value from the relationship any longer. It's not fair to either of you pretending that things are how they used to be—it's better for both of you to move on. Here are some key warning signs:

1. Most of your conversations are spent talking about past events instead of future possibilities.

2. You feel reluctant to share your dreams for the future, or worse, if you do they are cut down.

3. You are not genuinely interested in hearing about what they did on the weekend, and vice versa.

When a chameleon goes from a muddy brown swamp into a lush green jungle, the color of its skin changes—you guessed it—from brown to green. The change in skin color is a reaction to the environment of the chameleon. This is similar for humans, except that it is your attitude and ambitions taking on the appearance of the environment, not your skin color. As the mud of the swamp and the leaves of the jungle change the color of the chameleon, the people you associate with can change your attitude and ambitions.

> *There are two things that will make a huge difference to your life—the people you meet and the books you read.*
>
> —Charlie "Tremendous" Jones

The size of your dreams, the experiences you pursue, the choice of your major, your outlook on life and what you do on the weekend are all influenced by the people you associate with. It is important to be conscious of the people you choose to hang around and the influence they have on you. You choose to go from brown to green by the relationships you let go of and the relationships you foster.

If you want to be green, you must choose to be in a green environment surrounded by green people! What is the color of your environment? Is it the color you want? Is it the color you want for your future?

WARNING: The following types of people are hazardous to your health.

As you go through life you will have the opportunity to add many people to your network. Be careful of the following people because they can disturb your focus, drain your energy and prevent you from moving forward.

1. Negabots

Negabots are the easiest people to identify, and they are also the most toxic. A negabot is someone who is more often negative than positive. Negabots choose to see the negative side of things—their glass is always half empty, not half full. Negabots suck the positive energy right out of you, leaving you drained and feeling negative. Want a test to see if someone is a negabot?

Here's the simple test: wait for someone you suspect is a negabot to say 10 things. As he or she talks, count how many negative and positive things are said. If you count more than five negative comments, you have a negabot on your hands. If you count more than eight, run for your life!

2. Needy people

Needy people violate the eighth (and most important) rule to make everyone like you—they take WAY more than they give. They are always asking for favors and they are never satisfied—they always need something else. Needy people drain your time and your energy and offer you nothing in return. Do you hang with any needy people? Do you give into their constant requests?

3. Chaos-makers

Chaos-makers, as the name suggests, create chaos. They thrive on attention and feel important when associated with chaotic, traumatic or crisis situations. These people take a small, insignificant event like stubbing a toe, or forgetting to do one of seven questions on an assignment, and make it seem like the sky is falling.

Chaos-makers bounce from here to there creating havoc as they go. Take them in manageable doses, because they can easily disturb your focus and bring unnecessary chaos into your life. Spending your time with negabots, needy people and chaos-makers is hazardous to your health. They create unneeded tension and negative energy in your life, offering you little or no value in return. Do you have any negabots, needy people or chaos-makers in your network who need to be given the boot?

If you want to soar like an eagle, you better
stop hanging around with turkeys.

—Jim Rohn

The people you associate with have a significant impact on your life. Surrounding yourself with like-minded people gives you the support and encouragement you need to pursue your dreams. They provide you with opportunities they know you will benefit from, and they understand your greatest challenges and desires. Such relationships are the benchmark of solid friendships—ensuring anything you need is just a phone call away. Develop the habit of enrolling great people into your network. You'll never regret it!

CONCLUSION

In life, your opportunities come from *who* you know, not what you know. Likewise, who you know and who you hang with is a direct reflection of where you will end up.

Eight Ways to be Liked by Everyone

1. Make the other person feel important.
2. Before reacting to a situation, ask yourself, "What would it be like in their shoes?"
3. Let other people talk about what interests them.
4. Show appreciation where appreciation is due.
5. Remember names—it is everyone's most cherished word.
6. Smile often and greet people with enthusiasm.
7. Do what you say—no exceptions!
8. In your relationships, make more deposits than you do withdrawals.

The Three-step, Sure-fire Networking System

1. Make the contact through your network neighborhood.
2. Follow up via e-mail, phone or a thank-you card.
3. Add value by sending information, following through on a promise, sharing a contact or asking how you can help.

80/20 Rule of Your Network

- 80 percent of the value your network provides comes from 20 percent of the people.
- Figure out who these 20 percent are (your star list), and focus on building these relationships further.

You Are Who You Hang With

People to avoid:
- Negabots—people who are negative more than positive
- Needy people—people who take more than they give
- Chaos-makers—people who create chaos constantly

What does your network look like? Are your friends holding you back? Do the following Action Steps to find out.

ACTION STEPS

Online version available in *The Focus Zone* at:
www.focusedstudent.com

Who's On Your Team?

Add Someone to Your Network

Develop Successful Relationship Habits

Who's On Your Team?

Write the names of the five people you spend the most time with:

1. _____

2. _____

3. _____

4. _____

5. _____

Now, let's evaluate your team. Complete each of these steps and record your information in the chart on the following page.

1. Write down the top five names listed above in the top right section of the chart.

2. For each person, mark a ✓ or an ✗ beside each statement or question.

3. Total the number of ✓s for each person to determine their performance.

TEAM SCORE Fill in names into slots on the right-hand side	John Smith					
They are a positive person (not a negabot)	✓					
They give more to the relationship than they take						
They are not a chaos-maker	✓					
They support my ambitions and ideas	✓					
I see them in my life 10 years from now						
Total Scores	3					

4. Now make your star list. Anyone who scored four points or higher automatically goes on your star list. Also add those people in the 20 percent of your network who add 80 percent of the value, or more, to your life. There is no limit to the number of people, so write in the margin if you need more room.

_____   _____

_____   _____

_____   _____

_____   _____

_____   _____

_____   _____

These are the people in your life you should be focusing on, your value creators. In return, make sure you are constantly adding value to them.

To learn creative ways to add value to your star list, go to the online Action Steps in *The Focus Zone*.

Add Someone to Your Network

In the space below, write the name of someone you have recently met who you want to stay in touch with (the more recent the better).

_____

What information about them did you capture and how did you capture it?

_____

_____

_____

_____

When are you going to follow-up and what are you going to include in your follow up communication?

_____

_____

How are you going to add value to this person?

_____

_____

Develop A Relationship Habit

Use the successful habits formula to get rid of a bad relationship habit and replace it with a successful new one.

Habit That Is Holding Me Back	Successful New Habit	Three-Step Action Plan To Jump-Start My New Habit
EXAMPLE: Only hanging out with my close group of friends.	Meet one new person each week.	1. Face the fear of leaving my comfort zone 2. Have a conversation with one new person each day this week 3. Hang out with someone outside my group
Consequences if Continued	**Specific Benefits**	
- limited diversity in my network - have no friends if I go away for a summer	- have multiple social groups - will meet interesting people	**Start Date:** Friday, September 28
Habit That Is Holding Me Back	**Successful New Habit**	**Three-Step Action Plan To Jump-Start My New Habit**
		1. 2.
Consequences if Continued	**Specific Benefits**	3.
		Start Date:

Your Financial Future Starts NOW!

The main reason people struggle financially is because they have spent years in school but learned nothing about money.

—Robert Kiyosaki

Dick Marsden lay on the hospital bed, a broken man.
A heart attack 10 days earlier had almost taken his life. After running numerous tests, his doctor concluded that stress was the primary cause of the attack. As Dick reflected on his life, tears streamed down his cheeks. How could he have ended up like this: broke, disillusioned and alone? He was 67 years old, an age when he should have been enjoying retirement to the fullest with his wife, Jan, the love of his life for 42 years. Why had it all gone so horribly wrong?

Jan had finally left him two years ago, tired of the empty promises and the constant squabbling over money. He now realized—too late—that most of the turmoil in his life had been caused by financial problems. After graduating with a bachelor of arts degree, he had started work as a junior administrator for an engineering company in St. Louis. The salary wasn't great but it was a steady job with reasonable benefits. Dick thought about those early years, the fun times, attending ball games and parties with friends. Financial planning had never entered his mind. Life was pretty good, and retirement was light years away. Then Jan came along, a whirlwind courtship ensued, and suddenly Dick was married and settling into a familiar routine. Three children arrived quickly, and with Jan choosing to stay home, Dick had to work overtime to make ends meet.

Mortgage payments contributed to the growing financial pressure, and Dick's salary only increased marginally each year due to an uncertain economy. More than once he thought about going back to school to study environmental science. He had a love for nature and always wanted to work as an environmentalist, but the thought of starting over was too scary. He'd be making even less money and he was hardly keeping his head above water now. Dick continued in his steady job with no real future, living a lifestyle that day after day was sucking him dry financially.

At age 55, there was no freedom, only the thought of more work and an IRA account he had not contributed to consistently. The time to invest wisely had passed him by. Dick had sold Jan on a retirement dream, the two of them traveling the country in a luxury motor home, with all the time in the world and plenty of money to enjoy it all.

By the time he retired, Dick was just about broke. In a panic he had invested what little savings he had in a couple of get-rich-quick schemes that had bombed. That's when Jan walked out. Even worse, his children blamed him for the break-up. Soon they stopped coming to see him. Three weeks after entering the hospital, Dick succumbed to another heart attack. He died broke and alone.

Sadly, this is not an uncommon story. If you think we're trying to scare you, you're absolutely right, but it's for good reason. The U.S. Department of Health, Education and Welfare discovered depressing statistics that show just how common Dick's story really is. They tracked people from age 20 to age 65, finding that by age 65, for every 100 people:

- 1 was wealthy

- 4 were well-off

- 5 were still working because they had to

- 36 were dead

- 54 were dead broke—barely surviving off family or the government!

Enjoying the golden years has become a far-fetched reality for many, unless working in a gift shop is part of the retirement dream. Scarier still, people today are in a much worse financial state than people from Dick's generation. In the United States alone, the outstanding credit card debt sits at a whopping $700 billion, 14 times higher than it was in 1980! According to The American Bankruptcy Institute, since 2001 more young people declare bankruptcy each year than graduate from college. The statistics continue to worsen. What will the situation look like when your retirement day comes?

> *Today's average 50-year-old has only $2,300 saved toward retirement.*
>
> —J. Arthur Urtivoli,
> Sr. VP, Merrill Lynch

Unfortunately, due to the huge numbers of retiring baby boomers and increasing life expectancies, Social Security reserves are taking a beating and run the risk of being completely washed up by the time you retire. What are people doing wrong? What has caused this staggering situation to transpire? More importantly, why do *you* need to know about this now?

The problem is a result of two things: poor financial education and insufficient time. Poor financial education stems from a deficiency in the education system. In school we are never taught how to plan for a secure financial future. We do not learn how to create the financial future we want, nor do we learn how to leverage money so we can enjoy financial abundance.

Lack of financial education is also the root cause of the second issue—insufficient time. After college, with little education in financial planning, most of us start earning a living and jump on the Financial Treadmill—working, earning, then spending (we'll investigate the Financial Treadmill later). Soon enough, midlife rolls around, and we realize that we are not prepared for retirement. By the time this realization is made, a key player on our financial planning team has been lost—time. The less time we have to plan for our financial future, the harder it becomes. To support the increase in life expectancy, higher debt loads and diminishing Social Security funds, more planning is needed for our generation than for any other generation in history.

Don't panic—you're about to learn how to counteract this problem so you will be in the one to five percent of people who end up well-off or wealthy upon retirement, depending on your ambitions. You will learn two simple strategies to create the financial future of your dreams, whether you want to stop working at age 40 or 65. You will also learn the secrets of debt—how to minimize it, how to manage it and how to use it to fast-track your future success. **We are sharing these powerful principles with you now, because now is when your financial future starts.**

- Now is when you start shaping your financial habits.

- Now is the time you either invest in yourself with good debt, or dig yourself a seemingly inescapable hole of bad debt.

- Now you can learn the truth about money (that isn't taught in school) and avoid making mistakes like Dick.

- Now you can take advantage of time so you can create the financial future you really want with minimal effort.

Words of Wisdom from LES:
As a business coach it saddens and bewilders me to see so many "mature" people—those in their fifties and sixties especially—who are in a state of absolute panic because of money problems. PLEASE PAY ATTENTION TO THIS. No, paying attention isn't good enough—BRAND IT indelibly into your brain. Your financial habits *will* determine your future! That's not "maybe," "possibly," or "might"— the word is *will*. The reason millions of baby boomers in North America will be facing severe financial hardship in their senior years is simply because they never bothered to learn and implement good financial habits when they were young. Now is the time to begin. If you don't, you could end up as another forgotten statistic on life's financial scrap heap, with the label "BROKE!" hanging around your neck. Is that what you want?

It's time for money talk. No matter if you want loads of money so you can have a yacht and three Ferraris, or if you just prefer to be comfortable, this focusing strategy will teach you how to create the financial future you want. Consider this the start of your financial education. Don't worry: it won't be like a boring math class where you need an overpriced calculator to solve complex formulas. These concepts are simple, yet powerful. They will show you exactly how to create wealth, regardless of what career you choose.

Choose The Financial Future YOU WANT

Two options exist for creating a sound financial future. The first option is focused on **retirement**. The second option is focused on **financial freedom**. Both options are founded on the strategy called **pay yourself first**, which is arguably the most fundamental piece of financial advice ever given. Paying yourself first is a simple system for using the money from your hard-earned income to build yourself an abundant financial future. Here's how it works:

1. Take a small portion of each paycheck (10 to 15 percent) and set it aside in a Pay Yourself First Account.

2. Spend what's left on paying bills, supporting your lifestyle and contributing to worthy causes (rent, car payments, utilities, entertainment, charities, etc.).

3. As your Pay Yourself First Account grows, put the money into investments.

Do millionaires do this? We're glad you asked. Thomas Stanley and William Danko, authors of the international bestseller *The Millionaire Next Door,* found that the average millionaire puts 15 percent of their income into a Pay Yourself First Account. So yes, this strategy is tried, tested and taught by the richest people on this planet. Paying yourself first takes little effort and quickly becomes a habit. With self-discipline, you'll be surprised how easy it is to live off 85 to 90 percent of your salary—most people don't even notice the difference.

> *Every fortune in this world began*
> *with a balance of zero.*
>
> —Suze Orman

What you do with the money in your Pay Yourself First Account is the major difference between option #1, retirement, and option #2, financial freedom. You might be thinking: "Wait a minute, you want me to put away 10 percent of what I earn. I can barely afford to eat!" Starting to pay yourself first while still in college is not feasible for many students, especially if you have zero income. Don't sweat it. The key is to understand that paying yourself first is the foundation of your financial future. When you start earning income (even if it's not until after college), you can start paying yourself first. As you are about to learn, the sooner you start using this principle, the sooner money will no longer be an issue for you.

Financial Future Option #1
RETIREMENT

Retirement is living off your savings and investments after you decide to stop working. This option is for those who want to retire comfortably around the age of 65 and take a hands-off approach to investing. This doesn't mean putting the money from your Pay Yourself First Account into investments carelessly. It means putting the money into investments that take less time, expertise and management. These types of investments typically offer small returns, are longer term and are managed by a third party such as a financial planner, the bank or the government. Here are a few common examples of these low-involvement investment options:

- **401K:** retirement plans offered by your employer that have special tax advantages

- **IRA:** individual retirement accounts that have special tax advantages (similar to an RRSP in Canada)

- **Bonds and certificates:** lending your money to a company or government for a specific period of time in return for earning interest on your money

- **Mutual funds:** a collection of stocks and bonds chosen and managed by a professional

These investments are typically your safest options, but as a result they also offer a lower return and are usually locked away for a specific period of time.

To use these hands-off investments to create a secure financial future, one critical thing has to happen. Do you know what it is? It starts with the letter C and was acclaimed by Albert Einstein as "the eighth wonder of the world and the most powerful force on earth." If you guessed computer, you guessed wrong.

The combination of time and compound interest is more powerful than a locomotive, a nuclear reaction, or even a Tony Clark home run.

—David Chilton

The answer is compounding. The following four steps will show you exactly how option #1 works—from paying yourself first, to using the money to invest in hands-off investments, to letting your money compound until you are ready to retire.

Step 1: Pay Yourself First
Take 10 to 15 percent of your income and deposit it
into your Pay Yourself First Account.

Step 2: Invest
Take the money from your Pay Yourself First Account and put
it into hands-off investments such as those listed on page 221.
For compounding to take effect, the money invested and
the investment income it earns must be allowed to grow.
It can't be spent. So keep your paws off it!

Step 3: Let Compounding Do Its Magic
Why did Einstein, one of the most intelligent men of all time,
acclaim compounding to be the eighth wonder of the world?
Because it's one of the few ways to make your money work
harder than you do. It's an easy way to become a millionaire
and a convenient way to build a substantial retirement fund—
that is, if you start now and put time on your side.

Compounding is incredibly simple. Rather than spending
the interest you earn on your investments, you re-invest this
money so your investment account grows by a larger amount
each year. You earn interest on the original money you put in
and on any interest earned on that money. In other words, you
get paid interest on interest! As you continue to invest year
after year, your retirement account will grow exponentially due
to the magic of compounding. Sound confusing? If you don't
quite get it, keep your eyes peeled for the upcoming graph—
it will give you a great visual of the compounding effect.

Step 4: Retire
Once you accumulate enough money to support your
desired lifestyle for the remainder of your life, you can
stop working and start your golfing or gardening career.

How much money will you have upon retirement?
Let's say you earn $40,000 per year, put 10 percent in your Pay
Yourself First Account every month and receive an average
return of 7 percent on the hands-off investments. If you start

at age 23, how much will you have at age 65? The answer is $1.2 million! However, if you're a bit lazy and start at age 35 you will have only $600,000. By waiting until you are age 35 to get started, you cut your retirement savings in half! Obviously, you need to start early if you want to take full advantage of this eighth wonder of the world.

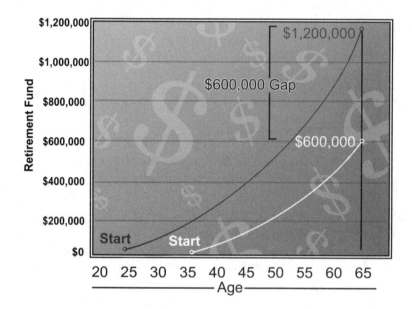

So now you're 65 years old, retired, and you have $1.2 million in your bank account. What happens next? Like it or not, you have entered a race—a race between your bank account and your life. What most people won't tell you is that the race involves two unpleasant characters—Mr. Tax Man and Miss Inflation. The key is to understand how much Mr. Tax Man will take and how much Miss Inflation will discount your money so you can prepare for the race accordingly.

With a retirement fund of $1.2 million dollars at age 65 and applying average tax and inflation rates, you will have about $30K per year until age 89, $40K per year until age 80, or $60K per year until age 74 (remember, this is after-tax money and adjusted for the future). If living off $30K per year until you are 89 requires a retirement fund of $1.2 million, imagine the financial strife of those with a retirement fund in the mere thousands. Scary stuff. Therefore, the more extravagant retirement lifestyle you want, the bigger retirement fund you will need . . . and a million dollars isn't as big as it sounds. To increase the size of your retirement fund, you can:

- put more than 10 percent of your paycheck into your Pay Yourself First Account

- reap higher returns on your investments by learning about higher-return investment options (such as real estate) and becoming more involved in your investment decisions

- most importantly, start earlier. Simply starting a few years earlier can produce hundreds of thousands of dollars you would otherwise not have

Treasure #7 at *The Focus Zone* at focusedstudent.com is a Riches at Retirement calculator. Use it to determine how much of your income you need to put in your Pay Yourself First Account and what returns you require to have a multi-million dollar retirement fund in your 40s, 50s, 60s . . . or whatever retirement age you want to shoot for.

> *Money may not make you happy, but lack of money*
> *can certainly make you miserable.*
>
> —David Bach

Financial future option #1 is a great option for those who want to retire comfortably and take a hands-off approach to investing. If you choose this option, remember that time is your key ally, and that starting sooner will allow you to retire much earlier, with much more money. Also, don't overlook taxes and inflation. You will be in a race with your bank account, so make sure you are putting away enough money to allow your bank account to win the race. Until you retire, you will also be stuck on a Financial Treadmill (often called the rat race). It is important to learn about the Financial Treadmill now, so you can determine if it is something you are willing to endure or if you would like to get off the treadmill by choosing financial future option #2.

The Financial Treadmill

The Financial Treadmill is the endless cycle of work➔ earn ➔ spend. You are on the Financial Treadmill if you trade your time working to earn a salary. If as you earn more you spend more, then you'll have to keep working more (running on the treadmill) to maintain your lifestyle.

The Financial Treadmill isn't necessarily a bad thing. If you have passion for what you do, enjoy your career and are confident you will be satisfied working until you retire, the Financial Treadmill may not bother you at all. For many, the idea of working an enjoyable job until retirement at the age of 60 or 65 sounds like a solid plan. If that appeals to you, then financial future option #1 is a great solution.

© The Power of Focus, 2005. CASEY JOHNSON

Other people don't like the idea of being bound to a treadmill (a job)—they want more free time to enjoy their lifestyle; they want more time to spend with family and friends and they want the option of switching careers at ease without ever having to sacrifice their standard of living.

Option #1 is a great way to create a comfortable retirement with little effort. However, the Financial Treadmill is a part of the equation and is something you'll have to endure. Option #2 is about getting off the Financial Treadmill and achieving financial freedom. If you want the big bucks you better hang on tight, because option #2 will show you how to become as wealthy as you desire!

Financial Future Option #2
FINANCIAL FREEDOM

This option is for people who want substantial wealth to share with others, lots of free time and riches before they wrinkle. **To succeed with this option you must be willing to continually increase your financial intelligence and take the time to put what you learn into action.** You will still need to use the "pay yourself first" principle. The difference is that the money in this account will primarily be used for hands-on investing that requires your time and knowledge, at least initially. Another fundamental difference between the two options is that in option #2 there is no such thing as retirement. Instead of retiring, you reach financial freedom.

What is financial freedom? Financial freedom is having enough money to live the lifestyle you desire and do what you want with your time. The difference between retirement and financial freedom is that retirees live off their limited retirement fund, while those who are financially free live off continuous streams of income. These streams of income are known as passive income.

Do You Know What Wealth *Really* Means?

Society often defines wealthy people as those with
a big house, a big paycheck and a cherry red Porsche
on the driveway. This definition is false.

Wealth is not measured in material possessions. In fact,
wealth is not measured in dollars, euros, pounds or yen.
Wealth is measured in time. Your level of wealth is
determined by the amount of time you can live your
current lifestyle without ever working again. How wealthy
are you? How wealthy do you want to be?

Let's look at the two types of income—active and passive.

Active Income

Active income is income you make through working actively—
an hour of work for an hour of pay. The more hours you work,
the more money you take home; miss work and you don't get
paid. Active income is distributed in the form of a paycheck, tips
or commissions. It is the most common way to earn a living.

Passive Income

Passive income is different from active income because it isn't
directly proportionate to your time; it is money earned with
very little time invested. It is income you generate while
you sleep. For example, if you buy a house and rent it out for
$1,000 per month and your monthly expenses for owning the
house (mortgage, taxes, insurance, etc.) cost you $600, then
you are receiving $400 per month in passive income ($1,000
- $600). You might have to swing by and collect rent checks
or make sure the tenants aren't trashing the place (especially
if you're renting to rowdy students), but in general you
are making income that isn't directly proportionate to your
time—passive income.

Passive income slows down the Financial Treadmill. The more passive income you earn, the less you have to work for active income to maintain the same lifestyle. By generating enough passive income to cover your living and lifestyle expenses you can stop the treadmill completely and end the days of trading your time for a paycheck. You are then free to do whatever you want with your time knowing passive income checks will continue rolling in each month.

The Myth of the High Paying Job

The ultra-wealthy focus on creating multiple streams of passive income rather than focusing on earning a high salary through active income. By viewing wealth through this lens, you will notice that many highly paid individuals such as doctors, senior executives and investment bankers aren't as wealthy as they appear. They are on the same Financial Treadmill of work➔ earn➔ spend as those with salaries half the size.

If they wanted to become truly wealthy, they would need to generate passive income so they could work less and still live the same lifestyle.

Here comes the good news. No matter how big or small your paycheck is, anyone can generate passive income. By putting 10% or more of your active income into your Pay Yourself First Account and then using that money to generate streams of passive income (we'll show you how in the next section), anyone with any salary can get off the Financial Treadmill and become financially free.

If you choose to follow this wealth secret and begin to build passive income streams, you will eventually generate enough passive income to cover your entire living expenses. When your passive income consistently exceeds your expenses you are (drum roll, please . . .) financially free!

> ## The Financial Freedom Formula
> ## PASSIVE INCOME > Expenses

When you are financially free, you no longer need to work for active income (a job) to cover the costs of your lifestyle, because your passive income covers all of your lifestyle expenses. You can then use your time to do whatever you please. What happens when your expenses go up? It isn't the end of the world—just ensure you raise your passive income so that the financial freedom formula (passive income > expenses) still holds true.

Achieving Financial FREEDOM

Air'n Monahan started college with $130,000 in scholarships. He discovered a simple system for winning scholarships that his classmates didn't even know existed. Realizing how valuable his scholarships secrets were, Air'n became inspired to share them with others. Being a big thinker, he wanted to reach students beyond his local campus. He wanted students from coast-to-coast to have access to this information, so he set out to find a way to make it happen.

It wasn't long before Air'n realized the internet was his best option. He had discovered several websites that sold downloadable e-books and became excited by this business model. He scheduled a few hours away from his studies, invested a few hundred dollars from his scholarship money and began creating his own website and the e-book, *Scholarship Secrets*. He put in a lot of hours—unpaid hours—and spent additional hours learning the ropes of internet marketing. Less than two semesters later, his efforts paid off as he finished his e-book and launched his first online business. Within hours of being listed in search engines, Air'n began receiving orders. At first he managed the orders himself, but after another month of work his website was completely automated. In his first month Air'n made $352, his second $1,104, his third $2,870 and by the end of his first year he was making between $15,000 and $20,000 in revenue per month—100% hands off! This website—started from his dorm room—made Air'n financially free before his Senior year.

Air'n Monahan became financially free by creating a profitable online business. Yes, in the beginning there were long hours and little payoff for his time. However, Air'n saw it as a minimal effort for the reward of never having to search for a job again and having the freedom to do whatever he wants with his time. He admits that living on $15,000 a month isn't too shabby either. To become financially free you must pay yourself first and use this money to create passive income streams. Air'n used a small portion of his scholarship money to create an income producing website. What will you do?

Although there are hundreds of ways to generate passive income, we've learned first-hand that it's a different ball game when you're young, ambitious and broke. So, to help you streamline your search, we have included in this next section **the top four vehicles for creating passive income as a young adult.** If you're serious about becoming wealthy, this section and its treasures will help you take the next steps.

Passive Income Vehicle #1 – Online Businesses

Air'n Monahan's success is a perfect example of the potential that online businesses offer. Our generation has a huge advantage in the online world. We were practically born with keyboards at our fingertips. Our grey-haired teachers and parents may have more "life" experience, but they don't have a chance against us young bucks when it comes to computers.

There are several ways you can use your computer skills to create passive income. One option is to do as Air'n did and sell a product or service online. To help determine what product or service to sell, start by looking at your Passion Puzzle™ (page 64). What are your top interests and skills? What products or services could you sell on a website that that are in line with your interests or could teach others a skill you have mastered? For example, if you play the Saxophone you could look into creating an e-book or audio course that teaches others the basics in getting started. Once you have a few ideas, run them through the following three-question quiz to test their potential:

1. Is there a substantial amount of people searching online for related products or services?

2. Is there an opportunity in the online market for my product or service? (or is there a lot of competition)

3. Can this product or service be easily downloaded from a website or shipped from a distribution center without consuming my time?

If you answered 'yes' to these three questions, your idea could be the next online business success story. Anyone with basic computer skills can be successful at this, however you will need some basic instruction to get started. To discover how you can get step-by-step instruction to create your own online business and to see the website that is making Air'n $15,000 a month, check out www.StudentMoneyMachine.com.

Passive Income Vehicle #2 – Network Marketing

Network marketing is selling a pre-existing product through word-of-mouth and building a team under you who do the same. Because you earn a percentage on the sales generated by the people under you, passive income is produced. If you take off to Tahiti for a year, your business will continue making money—it might even pay for your entire vacation—as long as the people under you, and the people under them, keep doing their thing. To highlight the potential this business model offers, we interviewed Dale Sarna, a successful young guy who became financially free running his own network marketing business in college. Here's what Dale had to say:

> Although I was majoring in Accounting, I had a hunch that entrepreneurship was more my cup of tea. Network marketing gave me the opportunity to explore entrepreneurship virtually risk free. The cost to get started was very small and the business tools and training I received were outstanding! It was like a business in a box. I got my own website, business cards, marketing tools, and the rights to sell a world-class product endorsed by Olympic athletes. The network marketing company I joined gave me everything I needed to run a successful business, including access to mentors who taught me step-by-step how to achieve financial freedom in this business. Within the first six months I had made more money than I did in my prior two jobs combined. I'll never forget returning from a spring break trip in Cancun to find a check for $1,400 waiting for me. I had earned it passively while sipping Pina Coladas and playing beach volleyball in Mexico. That did it for me. I become incredibly passionate about helping other students learn about passive income. The more students I helped the more money I made. Graduating with no debt and being financially free was pretty amazing, but the biggest rewards were gaining confidence as an entrepreneur and seeing the success of the students I helped.

Dale's success came as a result of his integral approach to this business. He focused on helping students rather than selling to them. His success is proof of how important this approach is when choosing to get involved in network marketing.

Unfortunately, there are many people who have done a disservice to this brilliant business model. Being attacked by friends or family with overly aggressive sales presentations is one of the common turn-offs. There are also a lot of network marketing companies that go belly-up due to inferior products or an inexperienced management team. The good news is, network marketing has advanced significantly in the 21st century. New compensation models and online marketing systems have allowed this business model to become more attractive than ever before . . . especially for young people who are always online and connected to thousands of other students.

As Dale's story proves, success with this model is based on helping others become successful. The more people you help, the more successful you will become. **Be warned**: there are many network marketing companies that still operate in an old-school tacky fashion. If you question the quality of their product or feel like they use an aggressive sales model, then keep looking. To be successful in network marketing it is essential that you find an integral company (ideally one that is publicly traded) that has created an exceptional product.

There is not enough room in this chapter to give you the full-meal-deal on how to find good network marketing companies. There is a specific set of criteria that you will want to use and it can be found in this next treasure.

Treasure #8 in *The Focus Zone* at *www. focusedstudent.com* contains a free e-book entitled *The Ultimate Passive Income Producer—a young adult's guide to starting smart in network marketing*. This e-book is a must-read if you are considering network marketing. In addition to discovering the ten characteristics that create highly profitable and integral network marketing companies, you will also find out what Donald Trump has to say about this industry. Check it out.

Passive Income Vehicle #3 – Real Estate

If you own property where the rental income is more than the monthly expenses, you make passive income. Real estate is one of the most exciting ways to invest because it offers many additional perks:

Real Estate Perks

SOMEONE ELSE PAYS YOUR MORTGAGE: Your renters pay your mortgage, which leaves you as the owner of a paid-off property several years later.

THE POWER OF LEVERAGE: Buying real estate gives you the power of leverage. You can buy a house for $200,000 with as little as $10,000 in cash—or less. If you want to buy $200,000 worth of stock, for example, you must have $200,000 in cash.

PROPERTY APPRECIATION: Historically, real estate seldom goes down in value. The average property appreciation rate in North America sits around 5 percent per year. If you own a $200,000 property that only appreciated by the average rate of 5 percent, you would make $10,000 in one year in appreciation alone.

BUY BELOW MARKET VALUE: You can make big bucks by buying smart. By doing your homework you can buy a property for $200,000 that could easily be worth $220,000 or even $250,000. Properties are often sold below market value because of motivated sellers, divorce situations and inaccurate appraisals.

Buying a house may seem out of reach while in college, but rest assured it isn't. There are many ways to create passive income through real estate, and buying your own college pad is definitely one of them. You can start small by reading a book or you can learn hands on by attending a seminar or taking a course offered by a company like Trump University.

ANDREW:
It was a typical evening during my junior year. I was studying hard and out of nowhere I had an epiphany! At the time, I was sharing an apartment and paying around $400 per month for my room, which was slightly bigger than a shoe-box. I had been reading the book *Rich Dad, Poor*

Dad and was becoming ever more intrigued by passive income and real estate. I put aside my textbook and started crunching some numbers.

I realized that whoever owned these apartment units was making serious cake. Why was I paying someone else's mortgage AND putting extra money in that person's jeans? At first, I didn't think buying my own property was possible, being a starving student and all. However, as the months went on I realized that purchasing a property was much easier and more affordable than I had assumed. All I needed was a small percentage of the purchase price to buy the house and a few renters to cover the mortgage. A couple of real estate books, a weekend seminar and a whole lot of house shopping later, I had purchased my first property—just in time for senior year. I lived in the house and rented the additional rooms to a few friends. After a little redecorating (an automated disco ball, a foosball table, a beer-dispensing pop machine . . . you know, the usual student amenities) it quickly became the most popular house on the block—creating a waiting list of potential tenants willing to pay premium rent. I was getting $2,000 per month in rent and only paying $1,400 in expenses. My first passive income stream was working!

Three close friends were also dabbling in real estate, and they were interested in joining forces. Within a year we formed a corporation and owned just shy of a million dollars in property. Looking back, I would have laughed if anyone had told me I could own properties while still in school. That year I learned a valuable lesson: what seems out of reach will remain out of reach—until you start reaching for it.

Did you know that 80 percent of *all* millionaires made their first million in real estate! If you want six zeros in your bank account, check out Treasure #9 at focusedstudent.com for a free download of the e-book *Riches through Real Estate—A beginners guide to becoming a savvy investor.*

Passive Income Vehicle #4 – Trading

Trading is an exciting way to build wealth, especially for young people interested in investing. Everyone has heard of the stock market, but other popular markets also exist include trading currency, commodities and bonds. Each has its own market of buyers, sellers and ever-changing market conditions. We asked our friend Nathan, a 24-year-old trader who started trading back in college, to share what life as a trader is like.

> Trading is a philosophical art form that uses logic to analyze a market. First you choose a market, for me that was currency. If you are able to stay present in the face of fear and greed while staying disciplined enough to follow trading rules of your market, you can become a profitable trader. To be successful in trading, like anything else, requires hard work and determination—it's not a get-rich-quick game. The best way to get started is to choose a market, learn all you can from other traders, read several books on the topic and then do simulation online or get a demo account.
>
> If trading becomes a passion for you, then stay focused and never give up, because it is passion and persistence that lead to success in this game. Financially, trading can be very rewarding. I earn enough money in four hours a day of trading to allow me to spend the rest of my time enjoying life however I want.

For links to online trading simulations, recommended books and great courses to help you get started as a trader, go to www.StudentTraderZone.com.

Whether it's through online businesses, network marketing, real estate or trading, you can earn enough passive income to become financially free at a very young age. To join a club of like-minded young adults who are using these passive income vehicles to become financially free before their 40th birthday, go to www.Freedom39CLUB.com for more information.

Financial Future Option #3
SPEND MORE THAN YOU EARN

If you don't choose option #1 or option #2 and don't pay yourself first, there is a high likelihood you will be suckered into option #3. For many, option #3 is an irresistible offer, one that is too good to pass up. It is an appealing offer because it allows you to consume more today and have an improved lifestyle immediately. Unfortunately, this offer also guarantees a future of financial struggle.

SPECIAL OFFER

Financial Hardship Can Be Yours!!!

Want to struggle financially? Jump on the bandwagon! Millions of people have already discovered this timeless formula for financial chaos. You too can apply this simple formula and begin living a life of STRESS, HARDSHIP and FINANCIAL UNCERTAINTY!!! All this can be yours if you follow the simple formula below.

Expenses > Income

**That's right. All you need to do is
Spend more than you Earn!**

"After graduating from law school I immediately started using this formula. I bought a brand new car, rented a swanky bachelor pad and began living like the other high-priced lawyers at my firm. I was spending $100K a year and earning closer to $80K. Sure enough, the formula worked and I am now struggling to make my credit card payments."

—Bill Overdue, Debt Valley, Nevada

> HOW MUCH YOU EARN DOESN'T MATTER. ANYONE WHO APPLIES THIS FORMULA WILL STRUGGLE FINANCIALLY—**GUARANTEED!**

For more enjoyment, play the game "Keeping up with the Joneses." Wait for your neighbor (or a friend) to purchase something they cannot afford, then make an even larger, more irrational purchase yourself. **The person who has their house foreclosed first WINS!**

Don't wait. Start planning your disastrous financial future today.

Sadly, the majority of people in North America have fallen for this special offer—the statistics prove it. The percentage of disposable income spent on personal debt payments skyrocketed from 8.6 percent in 1980 to a whopping 84 percent in 1997. Think about that for a minute—84 percent of people's income is used for debt payments! Furthermore, the average American has over $8,000 in credit card debt alone.

Don't get suckered into this offer—pay yourself first, and whatever you do, don't spend more than you earn.

The option you choose is entirely up to you. If you choose the retirement option and let your money compound, or the financial freedom option and start developing passive income streams, two critical ingredients that are essential for your success are TIME and ACTION. The sooner you take action and start applying these principles, the sooner you will have the financial future of your dreams—and the easier it will be to create it.

Good Debt vs
BAD DEBT

The journey to financial abundance is not something that starts after college—it starts *in* college. College is where you start forming good (or bad) financial habits. It's where you make big decisions that can leave you with an overwhelming debt load or a bright financial future.

The large majority of students live in the land of debt, where cash is an endangered species. However, debt doesn't need to be a bad thing. Debt is how most people get started—funding a college education, starting a business or buying their first home or rental property. The trick is to recognize the difference between debt that will help launch you forward and debt that will forever hold you back. Let's show you what we mean.

There are two types of debt out there: good debt and bad debt. **Bad debt** is debt that will never provide a financial payoff. Examples include taking out a loan to buy a car, using your credit card to buy overpriced designer shoes or borrowing thousands of dollars from a sibling to mount a plasma TV above your bed. The money used to purchase these items will never be recovered. In many cases, especially with cars, these items will depreciate and need maintenance, taking more and more money out of your pocket.

On the other hand, **good debt** is debt that will give you a current or future financial payoff: a mortgage on a rental property, paying to attend an event that helps you land your dream job, buying art supplies that help you showcase your talent or attending an investment seminar to kick-start your journey to financial freedom. These are examples of good debt. Good debt creates an immediate or future payoff that exceeds the present cost.

GOOD DEBT	**BAD DEBT**
Debt that produces income for you	Debt that does NOT produce income for you
Cost of debt < payoff it creates	Cost of debt = NO financial payoff

Debt in any form—good or bad—is dangerous when used excessively. While in college, the key is to manage your levels of good debt and minimize your levels of bad debt.

Minimizing Bad Debt
IN COLLEGE

It's impractical to completely eliminate bad debt from college life. Buying new clothes and fixing holes in walls caused by your overly enthusiastic party-going friends is bound to happen. However, bad debt can easily sneak up and quickly turn into a mountain of consequences and limitations. Budgeting and avoiding credit card chaos are your two best solutions for keeping bad debt in check.

Budgeting

There is no right way to budget your money while in college, and there's no getting around how boring this topic is. We'll keep this short. The important thing is to have some sort of budgeting system that works for you.

LUC:

In my first year of college, when I heard the word budget, I thought of a car rental company. As the semesters rolled by, my debt load continued to increase and I had very little to show for it. I needed to solve the mystery of where my money was going. I created a simple spreadsheet with the columns labeled as months and the rows made into spending categories: School, Recreation, Home, Transportation, etc. At the beginning of each month I would record what I could afford to spend in each category. The next step was asking a simple question with every purchase, "Can I get a receipt, please?" It soon became a habit. I got a receipt for everything, from my tuition to an ice cream cone. At the end of each month I would sort my receipts, total them up and record the totals on my spreadsheet. Updating my budget took me less than an hour each month, but the initial shock of some of my poor spending habits took months to get over. I was amazed to see how expensive it was to own a car—gas, insurance, parking, etc. I was also surprised that my entertainment and cell phone (fun-related expenses) were double what I had anticipated. Having a budget made me conscious of where my money was going. It put me in control of my spending so I could minimize my bad debt. That simple spreadsheet was my second step in taking control of my financial future—the first step was realizing it was my responsibility.

If you don't like the idea of asking for receipts, carry a notepad with you to write your expenses in. Yes, you will look silly doing this, but it will only take a couple of weeks to answer the big question: "Where is my money really going?" If you start the school year with a large bank balance, you could try putting this money into a savings account and have your bank deposit a certain amount of it into a spending account each month . . . voila, you have a monthly budget. Whatever method you choose, you need a budget in order to minimize bad debt, avoid stress, prevent poor credit and, in some instances, to prevent you from starving.

Budgeting is one of those all-important life skills that college gives you the opportunity to develop. It will take a little trial and error to find a system that works well for you, but if you don't start this trial-and-error process until *after* you graduate, just a few little errors multiplied could lead to bankruptcy or having your house foreclosed. Moral of the story: If you don't already follow a system for budgeting, start one today.

Credit Card Chaos

By now you have probably been bombarded with credit card companies offering everything from free t-shirts to affinity cards with your favorite sports team plastered on the front. That innocent little piece of plastic can offer terrific convenience, and it can help build a good credit rating. But beware—it can also be the epicenter of financial ruin and credit problems. Most students use credit cards to rack up bad debt. In return, they are stuck paying premium interest rates as high as 22 percent. On the other hand, if a bank sees you consistently using the credit card and paying it off each month, it will trust your ability to handle this credit. That means the bank will be more inclined to offer you credit in the future—perhaps for a mortgage on your first house, or a rental property, or as a loan to start a business. Credit cards can be your best friends, but they can also be your worst enemy—it depends on how you use them.

College is the best time to develop good credit card habits, so get one if you haven't already, but be careful how you use it. Here are a few tips for smart credit card spending:

- Pull the card out only if you need to—using your credit card to purchase anything and everything makes it harder to manage and easier to go over budget.

- Pay it off monthly—make a note in your day-planner so you don't forget (if you won't be able to pay off a purchase at the end of the month, ask yourself if the item is beyond your budget).

- At least pay the minimum amount due each month —if you don't, your personal credit will be in jeopardy and you will be slapped with a late fee (usually around $29!).

Does the thought of getting out of debt worry you? Worry no longer—Treasure #10 at *www.focusedstudent.com* is a proven nine-step system for eliminating debt from your life. Start applying this system now, or simply enjoy the peace of mind knowing you can use it later.

Managing Good Debt
IN COLLEGE

Your largest debt load in college will likely come from a student loan used to pay your tuition bill. Student loans can be good debt or bad debt—it depends what you do with them. Students who make the most out of the college experience are the students who discover their ultimate careers, develop funda-mental life skills and have exciting opportunities to choose from upon graduating. These students have used their loans to create future payoffs, and therefore it is good debt.

On the other hand, students who rush through school and focus on getting a degree (the degree-focused mindset) rather than maximizing the experience (the experience-focused mindset) usually end up with hollow hopes upon graduation rather than concrete opportunities. They have used the student loan to receive a glorified piece of paper, and they often end up unemployed or in a job they don't enjoy. The future payoff of the loan was less than its cost, making it bad debt. What will your loan be categorized as?

College offers many invaluable opportunities that will help you discover your interests, make valuable contacts and jump-start an exciting career. However, sometimes these invaluable opportunities cost money. Damn!—that dreaded M word again. This is where managing good debt comes into play. Invest in yourself.

LUC:
It was the second week of the summer semester, and my car died. I had $3,500 left on my student line of credit to last me until the fall. I knew my living expenses would be $2,500 and I was planning to put $1,000 towards a business plan competition in October. I debated whether I should spend my last $1,000 on another car or keep it locked away for the competition. It was a difficult decision, but I chose to brush the dust off my bike after convincing myself the exercise would do me good.

After only a week of riding I came out of school one day to find my lock in two pieces and my bike missing. I was devastated. I had gone from wheels to walking in less than a month! I was a busy guy and walking wasn't something I was used to including in my schedule. It was pure frustration, increasing by the day. Spending that $1,000 on a car, regardless of how rusty and hideous it may be, was sounding like a glorious solution. I dwelled over it for days, knowing the business plan competition was at stake. I opted to free up $50 to see if I could solve my transportation problem through another means. I was in a local bike shop when a silver gleam caught my eye.

It turned out to be an aluminum fold-up scooter with rollerblade wheels, the kind that kids zip around on. I envisioned myself rolling around campus, steering my scooter with one hand and waving to girls with the other—the image made me laugh and want to cry at the same time. I bought the scooter for $49—just under budget. Riding that scooter was hard on my legs and even harder on my self-image. Some people laughed, while others made not-so-funny comments, but I rode that aluminum fold-up scooter with confidence, knowing that it was the cost of investing in my entrepreneurial future.

Buying a car would have cost $1,000 and given me no future value, but the business plan competition had the potential to validate the budding business idea I had with Andrew and put it into action—and it did just that! Looking back, it was worth every push of that little scooter and more.

By choosing to go to college, you have chosen to invest in your future. If you want to make it the best investment possible, you will need to invest in more than your tuition. This might mean doing an exchange to Europe or Asia, volunteering once a week at your school, working for free during a summer, or attending a conference or competition. These activities usually come with a cost, which at first may seem unhealthy to your financial diet. Rest assured, if you invest wisely, you'll create a much healthier financial future.

When you THINK you cannot afford something try this . . .

When you see an opportunity to make an investment in yourself, but the price seems unaffordable, ask yourself this question:

"How can I afford it?"

By asking yourself this question you give your mind the opportunity to find creative solutions to your budget blues. If you immediately tell yourself that you cannot afford it, you eliminate innovative solutions.

Kick-Start Your Financial
FUTURE IN COLLEGE

Do you want to kick-start your journey to financial abundance? Although you may have a mound of student debt and no full-time job, it doesn't mean you need to put your financial future on hold. Here are a few ways you can get started today.

College Courses

You are not taught in college how to pay yourself first, or how to develop passive income and become financially free. However, most colleges offer courses on real estate, stocks, personal finance and similiar topics. These courses can teach you the basics and increase your confidence about investing. You will pay hundreds of dollars to attend investing conferences not affiliated with your college, so you might as well take advantage of these courses while they are covered by your tuition fees and give you credit towards your degree.

Cashflow Club

Do you like board games? If you want to put your passive income producing skills to the test, a great way to do this is playing the game CASHFLOW 101. There are many Cashflow clubs across the country you can join, or you can start one at your school. It's a bit like Monopoly, but the winner is the first one to become financially free. It's a great way to get a solid grasp on these principles and have fun at the same time. We play regularly. Go to www.richdad.com/pages/clubs.asp for more info.

Read Your Way to Riches

Accept the fact that college won't teach you everything you need to know about money—especially if you want to be rich. Reading is an inexpensive way to heighten your financial knowledge. For a list of our favorite finance books, see the Resource Guide. Unlike many college textbooks, these books cost less than $20 and can often be found at your local library.

Start Investing

Whether you prefer retirement or financial freedom, whether you're still in high school or working on your third degree, you can start now! Buy a house, purchase some stocks or bonds, start a small business, or get involved with a network marketing company. These are very realistic ways you can get started while in college.

Let us leave you with a few last words from one of our favorite finance authors—Robert Kiyosaki:

> "Often when I give speeches, I tell people that with each dollar bill that comes their way, they have the power to determine their destiny. You can too . . . the choice is yours—every day with every dollar you receive and every dollar you spend. This is an awesome responsibility and it's an amazing feeling of power. Your financial future is in your own hands!"

CONCLUSION

By applying the concepts in this chapter you can create any level of wealth you want. To make this easy, start NOW!

Develop the Pay Yourself First Habit
- Every time you receive a paycheck, put at least 10 percent of it into a separate account and use this money for investments.

Financial Future Option #1—Retirement
- Retirement is living off your savings and investments when you decide to stop working.
- This strategy involves focusing on long-term hands-off investments and uses the power of compounding.
- Plan wisely, so you can be confident that your bank account won't die before you do.

Financial Future Option #2—Financial Freedom
- Financial Freedom is having enough money to live the lifestyle you desire and do what you want with your time.
- To become financially free, you need to escape the work→ earn→ spend cycle of the Financial Treadmill by creating passive income streams.
- Once your passive income consistently exceeds your expenses, you are financially free.
- This option requires an increased level of investment know-how and is more hands-on than option #1.

Good Debt versus Bad Debt
- Good debt provides an immediate or future financial payoff.
- Bad debt is debt that will never provide a financial payoff.
- Minimize bad debt by budgeting and using credit cards wisely.
- Manage good debt by investing in yourself during college.

Kick-start Your Financial Future in College
- Get started now by taking courses on investing and finance, reading books, playing Cashflow 101 and starting to invest.

> To begin creating the financial future of your dreams, complete the powerful Action Steps that follow.

ACTION STEPS

Online version available in *The Focus Zone* at:
www.focusedstudent.com

Your Journey to Financial Independence

Invest in Yourself

Good Financial Habits

Choose a Financial Future Option

Which option interests you more: option #1 (retirement) or option #2 (financial freedom)?

_____

Get Started Now

Write down one thing you will do by the end of the semester that will take you one step closer to kick-starting the financial future of your dreams. If you prefer option #1, you might ask a finance teacher for advice on compounding low-risk investments. If you prefer option #2, you might buy a book on real estate, investigate a network marketing company or enroll in a Trump University course.

_____

_____

Invest in Yourself

List three opportunities you are thinking of pursuing (a conference, study exchange, etc.), their cost and the potential future payoff.

Opportunity:	Cost:
Potential Future Payoff:	
Opportunity:	Cost:
Potential Future Payoff:	
Opportunity:	Cost:
Potential Future Payoff:	

Select the opportunity that offers the highest potential future payoff. Ask yourself, "How can I afford this?" List 12 ideas below. Often, the last few ideas are where the most creative solutions are found.

Ideas of How You CAN Afford It

(Example: sell old football equipment, ride bike to school.)

1. _____   7. _____

2. _____   8. _____

3. _____   9. _____

4. _____   10. _____

5. _____   11. _____

6. _____   12. _____

Good Financial Habits

Use the successful habits formula below to axe a bad financial habit and to transform it into a good one.

Habit That Is Holding Me Back	Successful New Habit	Three-Step Action Plan To Jump-Start My New Habit
EXAMPLE: Spending $4 on a latte every morning.	Make coffee at home every morning.	1. Buy coffee beans 2. Buy a portable coffee mug 3. Make coffee before I leave home every day next week **Start Date:** Monday, February 7
Consequences if Continued	**Specific Benefits**	
- have less money for going out - will go over budget	- have more money for going out - get to sleep for an extra 10 minutes	
Habit That Is Holding Me Back	**Successful New Habit**	**Three-Step Action Plan To Jump-Start My New Habit**
		1. 2.
Consequences if Continued	**Specific Benefits**	3.
		Start Date:

Summiting The Mountain

*The future belongs to those who believe
in the beauty of their dreams.*

—Eleanor Roosevelt

Let's do a quick recap. In Focusing Strategy #2—*Ignite the Fire Within,* you began uncovering your values, interests, skills and ambitions—the components of your Passion Puzzle™— to help discover the careers for which you will have passion. In Focusing Strategy #3 you learned about the four career directions (employee, self-employed/business owner, professional and artist) and began deciding which direction is best for you. This is where your journey began. We hope at that point the fog in the valley started to lift, and you were able to see some interesting career options. Now, which mountain do you climb? It might take a few test hikes to see the one you are most passionate about, but you will eventually find your way. Focusing Strategies #4 to #8 provided you with tools to accelerate your climb—as you practice using them, turning them into habits, they will aid you on your journey.

This final focusing strategy is about the remainder of your journey. What else will make you fulfilled, satisfied and successful as you climb? What are you destined for at the summit?

In the 1860s, a Swedish scientist named Alfred invented dynamite.
This was a significant breakthrough as it made the business of blasting through rock a much safer experience. It was certainly a lot better than playing around with nitroglycerine, the previous method of choice. Alfred became incredibly wealthy—building factories and laboratories in 20 different countries and being recognized by world leaders for his revolutionary invention.

He had passion for his work, made obvious by his tremendous drive and achievement. Although Alfred seemed to have it all, a tragedy would soon prove otherwise. In 1864 his brother Emil died in a horrific explosion. Mistakenly, a French newspaper reported that it was Alfred who had been killed in the blast rather than his brother. As a result, Alfred had the rare opportunity to read his own obituary! Although it praised Alfred for his discovery of dynamite, it also mentioned how his invention equipped world armies with the strongest killing machine in history. Alfred, being a pacifist at heart, was deeply distraught. The last thing he wanted was to be remembered as the creator of a killing machine. All his success, all his fame and all his riches no longer mattered to him—they weren't worth this fate.

For the remainder of his living years, Alfred set out on a new path. His dream was to create an incentive that would continually inspire others to benefit mankind in positive ways.

When he died in 1896, to everyone's surprise he left behind 94 percent of his vast fortune for the establishment of five prizes—for peace, chemistry, physics, medicine and literature. Yes, this man was Alfred Nobel—an individual who reached his dream in a roundabout way and is now remembered more than a century later for the legacy of the Nobel prizes.

Living with passion led to the revolutionary invention of dynamite, which brought Alfred Nobel tremendous success both as a scientist and as a businessman. However, it wasn't until Alfred discovered his deeper calling—his true purpose and his dream—that he was able to reach the highest level of happiness and fulfillment—the summit of the mountain. Nothing was worth more to him than this magical sense of being, not even his vast fortune.

The process of self-discovery is a journey that does not end when you discover a career that gives you passion. Living with passion is simply fuel to help accelerate your climb, and although it will help you achieve significant levels of success and happiness, it won't get you to the summit. This doesn't mean you stop doing work that gives you passion, it simply means you will need something in addition to passion to keep you striding forward with enthusiasm. Like Alfred Nobel, you will reach a point in your life where you crave a deeper level of fulfillment that passion alone won't satisfy. To discover what will give you this ultimate sense of fulfillment, you must ask the question Alfred did: "What do I want to be remembered for?"

This focusing strategy will help you uncover the answer to this question by investigating your purpose and your dream. Living with purpose allows you to clearly see the mountain summit. This is where your dream lies and is where the ulti-mate level of happiness and fulfillment is realized.

> *Everything—a horse, a vine—is created for some duty. For what task then were you yourself created?*
>
> —Marcus Aurelius

At this point you might be thinking, "Hold your horses! Purpose and dreams? This stuff is a little deep; after all, I'm only 19 years old." Well, stop and think for a moment. What if you wake up one day at age 40, unhappy, dissatisfied with your career and feeling empty inside? It's called a midlife crisis, and in our fast-paced, high stress world, it has become more common than ever before. Can you think of a middle-aged relative or family friend who did something radical—bleached their hair, ran off with the mailman, or quit a high-paying job to breed hamsters? Those are obvious signs of a midlife crisis. Victims are usually people who crave more out of life but don't know where to find it. They were never taught about purpose, and they have yet to unlock the dream they are destined to pursue. Until they live with purpose, discover their dream and begin pursuing it, they will stay forever stuck, longing for more.

Here's the deal! You can drift for the first half of your life before making this shift, or you can begin your journey now. Before we examine the journey to the summit, let's first find out what living with purpose and living your dream is all about. It's not as far out as you might think.

Living With PURPOSE

Oxford University researchers have uncovered disturbing facts about our friends with big trunks. Yes, elephants. Reports state that, on average, zoo elephants live only half the life span of wild elephants, are more prone to aggression and are less capable of breeding. Moreover, 40 percent of zoo elephants display what these researchers call "repetitive movements that lack purpose." It doesn't take a rocket scientist to realize that elephants don't like living in cages. Living in cages is not what elephants were made for—their purpose is found living in the wild. When you take an elephant's purpose away, you rob it of its life. Unlike humans, who can buy a motorcycle or bleach their hair, elephants are left walking in circles or banging their trunks aimlessly against a tree—not a whole lot of fun!

Living with purpose is what keeps us strong, satisfied, happy and healthy well into our wrinkled years. It is what keeps us energized. Knowing your purpose is knowing what gives your life meaning. It is the answer to the question: "What am I on this earth to do?" It contains a spiritual dimension and is beyond material things. It is your own standard for success—not the standards of your parents, your friends or society.

Take a second to envision a woman living among the sick and starving in a poverty-stricken country. Can you see her? Does the word success come to mind? Probably not. But what if we told you her name was Mother Teresa? Mother Teresa was a superstar in the living-with-purpose league. Material possessions didn't define her success—she had her own definition: always caring for the lives of those in need. This was her purpose. Her strength to remain dedicated to this purpose in every waking hour of each and every day is a remarkable feat that has set her apart as a saint.

Purpose isn't something that is reserved for patron saints or adulthood. It is something you will crave sooner than you might expect. A study conducted in 2004 by the Roffy Park Research Foundation showed that 70 percent of young workers are looking for more meaning in their work—they are looking for purpose. Many people go through their entire lives never feeling fulfilled or excited about what they do because they fail to find their purpose—they are like elephants trapped in cages, which severely diminishes their true potential. What would it take for you to smile ear-to-ear all day long? What is the mark you were meant to leave on the world?

Living Your
DREAM

Do you have a dream? Of course you do, even though you might not know what it is yet. It's normal for dreams to seem outrageous, huge, on the verge of impossible. Dreams lie way outside our comfort zone. They involve taking on bigger challenges than ever before. If you're going to dream, why not make it a big one? It doesn't take any more energy to dream big than it does to dream small. There isn't a whole lot of excitement or stretching involved in climbing up a little molehill, is there?

© The Power of Focus, 2005. CASEY JOHNSON

"I wish I had pursued a bigger dream."

Before we show you how to discover your dream, let's look at a few famous dreamers and college students, just like you, who have discovered their dreams:

Famous Dreamer #1—Neil Armstrong
Dream: To travel to the moon

Famous Dreamer #2—Jennifer Lopez
Dream: To be a world-class performer

Famous Dreamer #3—Martin Luther King, Jr.
Dream: To bring freedom to African-Americans

Famous Dreamer #4—Coco Chanel
Dream: To revolutionize women's fashion

College Dreamer #1—Kelley Alexander, Boston College
Dream: To produce movies that inspire the human spirit

College Dreamer #2—David Tal, UCLA
Dream: To make hemp paper the new world standard in an effort to reduce deforestation

College Dreamer #3—Maria DeGrandis, McGill University
Dream: To work for the World Bank, helping stabilize the economies of developing nations

The major difference between people pursuing a dream and those who aren't is that dreamers wake up each morning with a mission—something to work toward that is in line with their purpose and makes them happy. Living your dream—reaching the summit—is where the deepest level of happiness and truest sense of fulfillment are found. Everyone has a dream, everyone can follow that dream and everyone can discover the dream inside them.

"Don't trample on a young girl's hopes and dreams, Roy."

I couldn't find the sports car of my dreams,
so I built it myself.

—Dr. Ferdinand Porsche

You now know what to search for to fill your hunger for happiness—simply knowing this puts you in control and far ahead of the pack. Go on, pat yourself on the back. And don't worry, no one expects you to know your purpose and your dream right this minute. It takes time. With a little patience and focus your purpose and dream will unfold.

The sooner you know what you
are searching for, the sooner
you will find it.

Are you ready to begin uncovering your purpose and the dream within you? In this next section you will learn about three things to focus on—the finish line, defining moments and convenient coincidences—that hold the clues on your path to discovery.

Focus and
DISCOVER

Discovering your purpose and discovering your dream both involve the same process. Your purpose drives your dream, creating a strong connection between the two. For example, if your purpose is to educate disadvantaged children, your dream may be to set up a series of schools in rural Africa. This dream to set up a series of schools in rural Africa is a specific project that fulfills your purpose of educating disadvantaged children. Do you see the connection? Alfred Nobel's purpose was to invent things that would benefit mankind.

His dream was to create the Nobel prizes to encourage others to do the same. You don't need to discover your purpose before you discover your dream—you might already know your dream but never thought of defining a purpose.

It is like the ongoing debate of which comes first, the chicken or the egg. It doesn't matter which comes first. If you know your dream you can work backwards to see the broader purpose it fits into. If you know your purpose you will soon find a specific project—a dream—with which to carry out your purpose.

Do you have a rough idea of what your purpose or dream might be? Discovering your purpose and dream all boils down to one simple thing called *focus*. By focusing on discovering your purpose and dream, you will begin to see hints and clues that you never saw before. Think back to when you, or someone close to you, got a new car. What happened as you drove that new car? Did you suddenly begin to notice other cars of the same make and model? You might have thought, "These cars are a dime a dozen—they're everywhere!" This is **the power of focus**. By focusing your interest on a single type of car, perhaps a Ford Mustang, your eyes magically begin to seek out other Ford Mustangs. When you focus on discovering your purpose and dream, you will start to become aware of what really makes you tick—things that were always there but weren't on your radar screen.

What does science say?

For those who prefer concrete answers, there is science behind this. There is a part of your brain called the Reticular Activating System—the RAS—that tells your brain what to notice.

So, if you want to become more aware of something, focus on it, and the RAS will start working on your behalf.

Go to *www.focusedstudent.com* to pick up your final treasure: Creating a Dream Manifesto. This is a powerful activity to help you define your dream.

Do you want to learn how to make this easier? By narrowing your focus on the following three things—the finish line, defining moments and convenient coincidences—your purpose and dream will emerge much sooner.

1. FOCUS on the finish line

Remember Alfred Nobel? He didn't realize until the latter stages of his life that being remembered as the inventor of dynamite was not the legacy he wanted to leave. If, like Alfred, you could read your own eulogy, what would you want it to say? What do you want to be remembered for? What would you want your parents, friends and colleagues to say about you? Think about this for a minute. You probably don't want to just take up space. In fact, your answer will likely be related to making a difference or filling some need in the world. By the way, you don't need to become a famous celebrity or inventor to have a purpose and pursue a worthy dream.

> Words of Wisdom from LES:
> A few years ago I met a man in a Dallas hotel who obviously lived with purpose. His purpose was simple—to give people positive energy and to make them smile. His job? Shining shoes.
>
> His passion for this work was obvious. When you stepped down from that big chair after your shine, the polish on your shoes was so good you could see your reflection in them. His name was George and he was a true artist, an ambassador of his craft. People left with a smile and a spring in their step after spending a few minutes with this amazing man. His average tip for a $3 shine was $5! George was so good I heard a sales manager ask, "Do you do groups?" He knew if George spent an

hour shining the shoes of every person on his sales team, which was gathering for a sales conference upstairs, he would create a ton of positive energy—which he did!

George is a great example of how you can find your purpose in simple things and live with purpose without ending up in the tabloids. By focusing on the finish line—the end of your life journey—you will tap into the deep feelings and discover what it is you truly care about. These are reflections of your purpose and insights into your dream.

2. FOCUS on defining moments

Do you ever have moments when you are overwhelmed with positive emotions? When you feel like a million bucks?

LUC:
For more than eight years I tutored students in various subjects. When one of my students would have a breakthrough with a concept, I'd feel fantastic! I realized that it wasn't the subject matter that I enjoyed—it was the teaching and mentoring. I enjoyed helping others understand concepts and ideas that would add value to their lives. Realizing that simple, yet powerful piece of information was the foundation for determining my purpose—to help others reach their full potential.

There is a name for these powerful moments—they're called defining moments. Next time you have a defining moment, analyze it to find out what components of the experience gave you that great feeling. The answer to that question will hold many valuable insights into what really drives you and will open the door to discovering your purpose and dream.

3. FOCUS on convenient coincidences

Have you ever randomly met someone who could help you achieve a goal you were working toward, or who could move you closer to something you really wanted? Do you ever think, "That was strangely convenient?" How about those times when a job, a much-needed helping hand or a new friend suddenly appeared at the perfect time? These are convenient coincidences. This is a *coincidence* that happens at (you guessed it) a *convenient* time when you are in pursuit of discovering or reaching your dream. It is the world, the universe, God or some other higher power stepping in to give you a hand. Think back in time—recognizing and remembering your convenient coincidences will give you clues to your purpose and dream.

The more you focus on discovering or achieving your dream, the more convenient coincidences you will encounter.

> *If you want something bad enough, the whole*
> *world conspires to help you get it.*
>
> —Madonna

Imagine you are blind and can't see the path that leads you to your dream, nor can you see the first steps you must take to achieve it. By focusing on finding your way, you are saying to the world that you want guidance and assistance on your journey. You *will* get a response; it may come in the form of meeting a certain person who can help you through a challenge, or it may mean coming across a piece of information that helps you make a better decision, or perhaps someone recommends a book (like this one) that sharpens your perspective. Convenient coincidences are your guideposts to your dream. Get in tune with them and you will stay on course. Ignore them and you will become lost.

ANDREW:
Crossing paths with Luc during a hiking trip in the summer of my sophomore year was a huge convenient coincidence. Not only did we have a similar purpose, but

we also had a similar desire to share a particular message with students. By the end of the seven-day hiking trip, we had come up with the idea for this book. Crafting our message into an actual book, being published and getting it into stores across North America was a journey that brought with it many additional convenient coincidences. One in particular really jived with me.

It was a weeknight, around 1 A.M., and I was doing a little research for a school project. I was getting ready to shut'er down for the night when I stumbled across a website that would keep me wide awake for several more hours. The website was *www.UofDreams.com*—an all-inclusive internship program that helps students discover and land dream jobs. As I studied the site I had a strange sense of clarity. Just reading the website gave me shivers. Something was telling me that attending this program was not an option—it was a necessity. I didn't know why. I wasn't looking to land a dream job—I was on track to write this book and start my own business. Nevertheless, I was overwhelmed with a feeling of nervous enthusiasm, like how you feel as a kid on Christmas Eve.

There was one major conflict. I was enrolled in a work-study program in Southeast Asia for the first half of the summer and I was going to Europe shortly afterwards on an exchange program. There were barely nine weeks between trips, and University of Dreams was an eight-week program. The chances of it falling in the exact eight weeks I could attend were next to none. I will never forget going to the next web page and looking at the dates. Lo and behold, the program started four days after I got back from Asia and ended three days before I left for Europe. I couldn't believe it. I figured it was meant to be.

To make a long story shorter, if I hadn't attended University of Dreams that summer you wouldn't be reading this chapter. Among many other things, it filled a critical void in our business plan, one that was essential to our success and to the message of this book. Some will see it as luck, but my gut tells me that this coincidence was way too convenient to be guided by my powers alone.

Understand that it is absolutely normal not to know your purpose and dream yet. You might have a few ideas, and if so, that is a great start. There is also a chance that you already have a strong idea about your purpose and dream—perhaps you've had a vision of this for several years. Regardless, your college days are a great time to continue the search. By taking advantage of the many new experiences offered in college (adopting the experience-focused mindset) you will learn a ton about yourself, and you will start to get a clearer sense of what really makes you spark. As you journey through college and into the real world, never forget that you have a unique purpose and dream. You deserve the fruits and fulfillment that discovering your purpose and dream will bring. Focus on the finish line, on the defining moments and on convenient coincidences, and your dream and purpose will continue to be revealed to you.

Take a minute to think of a few dreamers—Walt Disney, Lance Armstrong, Oprah Winfrey, Martin Luther King, Jr.— perhaps even a friend or family member. What do their journeys have in common? The rest of this focusing strategy will answer this question and show you how to stay on course so your name can be added to the Dreamer Hall of Fame.

The Journey to
YOUR DREAM

For years, Daniel "Rudy" Ruettiger was told he would not amount to anything.

It was ingrained in little Rudy that he was too short and too dumb, and that he lacked talent. But despite his torment, young Rudy had a dream that one day he would attend the famed

University of Notre Dame. Even wilder, he imagined himself playing football for the Fighting Irish! Not only did people laugh at Rudy's dream, they encouraged him to stop dreaming. After all, Notre Dame was reserved for the smart and well-to-do kids. And football, especially division-one college football, required tremendous athletic ability, something that Rudy didn't have. In the minds of the Ruettiger family, dreaming was limited to graduating from high school and going to work at the local oil refinery in Joliet, Illinois.

After graduating from high school Rudy gave up on his dream, following his father's footsteps to start a career at the local refinery. A few months into the job an unexpected tragedy occurred, one that would forever change Rudy's perspective on life. His best friend, Pete, was killed in an accident at the plant. Pete was the only person who ever encouraged Rudy to pursue his dream. A few days earlier Pete had surprised Rudy with a special birthday gift—a Notre Dame jacket, just like the ones the players wore. He told Rudy, "You were born to wear this jacket."

His dream rekindled, Rudy decided not to waste another day working at the oil refinery. The day after Pete's funeral he was off to South Bend, Indiana—the home of the Fighting Irish. He enrolled at Holy Cross Junior College and spent two years studying day and night to get the grades he needed to be admitted to Notre Dame. With little money and no support, Rudy found himself with nowhere to live. As a result he ended up sleeping in the maintenance room!

Then came the big test—applying for entry into Notre Dame. After weeks of waiting, his reply letter finally arrived. Ripping open the envelope with feverish excitement Rudy read the words—*application rejected*. He was devastated. All this hard work for nothing. Determined not to quit, Rudy recommitted himself and applied again—and again the letter came back: *rejected*! When the response to his third application arrived, he didn't even want to open the envelope. Rudy was terrified of the news it could bear and let it sit unopened for several days as he built up his courage to peer inside. Finally, the magic word he'd been praying for appeared—*accepted*!

Despite all of the obstacles Rudy had persevered. Nothing could stop him now—he was a student at Notre Dame, and it was only a matter of time before he would be dressing with the Fighting Irish football team. Again, through sheer persistence and a never-say-die attitude, Rudy finally made it as a walk-on player, which allowed him to practice with the team. He never missed a practice. And despite being physically pummeled every week due to his small size, Rudy never quit. He kept bouncing back for more, earning the respect of the Fighting Irish coaching staff and eventually, the players.

Rudy's big moment finally came. He had practiced with the Fighting Irish for four years, and on the last game day of his senior year he was asked to dress for the game. Proudly placing the famous gold helmet on his head, Rudy ran onto the field where a capacity crowd (including his family) roared him on. The story was now out. This short young kid with the heart of a lion was running on the field as one of the famous Fighting Irish.

All game Rudy sat on the bench waiting for his chance to get on the field. With the clock winding down and the Irish comfortably ahead, his teammates begged the coach to let him play. Chants of "Rudy, Rudy, Rudy . . ." echoed through the stadium. Dan Devine, the head coach of the 1975 team, finally relented and gave the order and sent him on with 27 seconds left on the clock. The crowd went wild. Rudy was living his dream, and in that one and only play he sacked the quarterback! To this day, Rudy is the only Fighting Irish player to ever be carried off the field.

So what's your excuse? There will certainly be resistance on the road to your dream, and you will need to step outside of your comfort zone on a regular basis. Remember, you are climbing a mountain, not strolling through the park. It is a challenging journey that will test your confidence, your determination and your deep-seated desire to reach your dream. You already possess most of what you need to overcome the challenges you will face, and what you don't already possess you will learn along the way. There are no shortcuts, but the journey up the mountain toward your dream has specific stages that you must go through. You are about to learn how to identify these stages so that you are not surprised by them, and so you can use them to make you stronger as you stride toward the summit. Bon voyage!

Stop
PEOPLE

As the name suggests, Stop People are the individuals who will attempt to stop you. They usually show up early in your pursuit or sometimes before you begin climbing. They come in many shapes and sizes: family members, friends, rivals, landlords, professors and bosses. The toughest ones will be those closest to you. The bigger your dream, the more Stop People you will encounter. Stop People have three major motivations:

1. They don't want you to fail
Parents and friends are notorious for safeguarding you by encouraging the less-risky approach. They do this because they care for you and don't want to see you fall flat on your face. Expect to hear things like, "It's too risky!" or, "You're too young!"

2. You are disturbing their comfort zone
When you stretch your comfort zone and make a change in your life, you bring change into the lives of those around you—sometimes positive, sometimes not. Any change is a

disruption to the comfort zone of those closest to you. You might be threatening their assumptions about success, their routine, their level of wealth or control, or their personal insecurities about not following their own dream. Rudy's desire to go to Notre Dame stretched the comfort zone of his family. When you make the step, expect responses like, "It's impossible!" or, "You can't do that!" or, in Rudy's case, "Ruettigers don't go to college."

3. They don't want you to succeed

There may actually be someone out there who is jealous, nervous or threatened by what might happen if you climb the mountain and plant your flag of happiness and success on the top. There are many movies, novels and songs written about these antagonistic types of Stop People—they are the ones who cut the brakes, take the cheap shot after the whistle or put sugar in your gas tank. They'll get in your face and say, "Over my dead body!" or, "You'll have to go through me first!"

> *If Christopher Columbus had turned back,
> nobody would have blamed him. If he had quit,
> nobody would know him.*
>
> —Anonymous

Once there was a pond of tiny frogs who set out on a mission.

The goal was to hop up the steps of a very high water tower and bathe in the purest water in the land. No frog had ever accomplished such a feat, although it was something they all dreamed of doing. The big day came and crowds of frogs from neighboring ponds gathered around the tower to watch and cheer on the dreamers. The journey up the tower began—stair by stair, hop by hop. No one in the crowd believed that the tiny frogs would make it to the top. "It's way too difficult!" they yelled. "They'll never make it!"

It was a sweltering day and the sun beat down on their backs as they climbed. One by one, the tiny frogs began collapsing. "It's too difficult!" the crowd yelled. "Turn back, you won't make it!" More and more tiny frogs got tired and gave up.

But one frog continued, climbing higher and higher and higher . . . this one wouldn't give up! Believing in himself, he endured the heat, and after a big effort he finally reached the top. Now he was cooling off in the purest, cleanest, most refreshing water any frog could ever dream of. So what sep a-rated him from all the rest?

As it turned out, this frog was deaf!

You have a choice: either allow Stop People to stop you from achieving your dream, or cover your ears and press on.

Surviving
THE COLD

Have you ever left the house on a cool day without a jacket, only to stand shivering at a bus stop or waiting for a ride? The first few minutes were probably the worst, until you realized that you would be out there for a while and had better learn to survive it. Getting past Stop People is only the first stage on your journey to the summit. There will be times when things take longer or are harder than expected, and when it gets really, really "cold." Your motivation and determination will start to freeze, and you will begin to question whether or not to go on. We call this phenomenon "The Cold." Many dreamers succumb to The Cold and retreat down the mountain—giving up their dream. But if you hang in there, you will survive. The Cold is tough, and it will tire you out physically and mentally. Try and think of a famous dreamer who didn't go through tough times to reach their dream. Ray Charles, Oprah Winfrey, Lance Armstrong . . . it's simply a part of the journey.

*Dreams mean nothing unless you're strong
enough to fight for them and make
them come true.*

—Bruce Springsteen

There is a reason for The Cold. It will help you develop the strength, skills and stamina needed to live your dream to the fullest. The Cold is a test. By surviving your encounter with The Cold, you pass the test and prove that you are capable and ready to achieve your dream. Rudy survived two years at a community college, two rejection letters and four years sitting on the bench. Will you survive The Cold?

Persisting Through
AVALANCHES

When you are hiking to the peak of a snow-covered mountain there is always the danger of an avalanche. Avalanches attempt to push you down the mountain and bury your dream—they are the major roadblocks and challenges you face along your journey. A few common avalanches include:

Lacking Resources
This could be the lack of money, time, qualifications, experience or contacts. Rudy didn't have the grades to get into Notre Dame, but he didn't let this avalanche bury his dream.

Physical and Emotional Illness
Poor health, injuries, loss of faith and greed can overcome you. Did Rudy let his small stature prevent him from playing for the Fighting Irish? Did Lance Armstrong let cancer prevent him from winning seven consecutive Tour de France titles?

Closed Doors
Before being published, the original *Chicken Soup for the Soul* manuscript was rejected 144 times! The authors, Jack Canfield and Mark Victor Hansen, never allowed the avalanche of closed doors to get in their way. With more than 85 titles in print, the *Chicken Soup for the Soul* series has now sold over 100 million books—making it the largest book series in the world!

Your ability to seek solutions, have faith and maintain focus will allow you to persist through the avalanches that attempt to bury your dream. As Jack Canfield says, "When they say no, you say next!"

The F Word!

For the determined traveler, failure is not an option.
Failure is a means to reaching the top. Failures are simply
stepping-stones up the mountain. To learn from one's mistakes
is to use these stepping-stones to move
you closer to your dream.

In the words of Robert F. Kennedy, "Only those who
dare to fail greatly can ever achieve greatly."

Is a fear of failure holding you back?

Smart travelers have a trusted friend, family member or mentor close by who can help them through the tough times that avalanches bring. Who can you trust to help dig you out of an avalanche?

Ready, Aim . . .
ACT!

As you begin the journey toward your dream (and work toward achieving individual goals along the way), there are a few things to keep in mind. **The most important lesson a traveler must know is that there is no replacement for action —experience, knowledge, passion, purpose and focus are of little value if not combined with ACTION.**

Your courage to take action will set you apart from others. Action creates results. Only you can affect how often you act and how you act.

You can't hire people to do your push-ups for you.

—Jim Rohn

As you venture up the mountain toward your dream, take the following Action Laws with you. If you remember to act in accordance with these basic laws they will assist you greatly on your journey.

Law #1—Act in contribution
A little law of the world states: Give and thou shalt receive. This law is so ancient and so important that it's a cornerstone of the Bible. Acting in contribution means giving genuinely out of joy and gratitude for all that you have. Contributions are gifts you give to the world. There are lots of ways to contribute—it doesn't need to be money. You can contribute your time by volunteering, contribute your talents to where they are appreciated and provide your expertise where it is needed. In return, the world will give gifts back to you: love, money, friends, knowledge, compassion and support. You will need these things on your journey toward your dream, so don't forget to give and to give with an open heart.

> *We make a living by what we get, but we make a life by what we give.*
>
> —Winston Churchill

Law #2—Act as though there is a way
Despite the circumstances or the obstacles, there is always a way. People who find a way are the people who act as though there always was one.

Randy spent a lot of time on the Mississippi River.
After finishing high school, it became his favorite hang-out spot. The pollution in the river had always bothered him, but he had never done anything about it. That all changed when one day he and his friend found a full-sized refrigerator lodged in the river bed. That was a defining moment for Randy—

he could no longer tolerate the pollution in the river. Randy's mission began. He set out to raise enough money to clean out hundreds of miles of the polluted Mississippi River. At first Randy had no idea where to start, but he soon devised a strategy. He called the largest companies in the area and asked to speak to the CEO. His request was answered by a laugh, a friendly way of saying, "Is this a joke?" Randy didn't let this get to him —he was determined to talk to the head honcho.

Randy's genuine approach and sheer determination shocked everyone he spoke with. He worked his way through the maze and into the CEO's office of some of the largest companies in the United States. In just six months, after a few big "pretty pleases" and many doors slammed in his face, Randy had raised more than $1.5 million. His determination led to the cleanup of more than 300 miles of the Mississippi River—one of the largest river cleanup projects ever undertaken! It all happened because Randy took action and believed there was a way.

Where there's a will, there's a way.

As Randy has demonstrated, somehow it can be done and the result you desire can be discovered and reached. It begins with a state of mind—believing it is possible. As you learned in Focusing Strategy #6, solution-focused people get what they want because they open their minds to possibilities. Don't worry if you don't have a complete plan before you start. No one has all the answers before they begin—that would be no fun! As long as you have the will to succeed, you will find a way to make it happen.

Law #3—Act as though you have a choice

Despite pressure from friends, parents or society, how we act, how we react and where we end up in life is always guided by one thing—our choices. Even in the gravest situations, no one can take the power of choice away from us.

Walter was always in a good mood.

When asked how he was doing, he'd reply, "If I were any better, I'd be twins!" Walter also used to say, "Life is all about choices. You choose how you react to situations. You choose how people affect your mood. You choose how you live life."

One day Walter was involved in a serious accident, falling some 60 feet from a communications tower. Doctors worked tirelessly during 18 hours of surgery to keep Walter alive —performing various operations to keep blood from clotting in his brain. Miraculously, they released Walter from the hospital three months later. Although a paraplegic, he was as full of life as ever. Six months after the accident, when asked about his condition, Walter replied, "If I were any better, I'd be twins!" Walter explained the experience. "As I lay on the ground, I remembered that I had two choices: I could choose to live or I could choose to die. When they wheeled me into the ER and I saw the expressions on the faces of the doctors and nurses, I got really scared. In their eyes I read, 'He's a dead man!' I knew I needed to take action. There was a big burly nurse shouting questions at me. She asked if I was allergic to anything. 'Yes,' I replied. The doctors and nurses froze as they waited for me to continue. I took a deep breath and said, 'GRAVITY!' Over their laughter, I told them, 'I am choosing to live. Operate on me as if I am alive, not dead.'"

Walter survived, thanks to the skill of his doctors, but also because of his amazing attitude—he chose to live!

You have a choice. Every day you decide to either build a future you want, or to drift aimlessly through life. You choose if you will discover your dream and if you are willing to stretch your comfort zone to reach it. You choose whether you end up with just a college degree or you make college the absolute best investment of your life. You decide whether your future is worth focusing on. These are choices only you can make—so what's it going to be?

CONCLUSION

In the quest for happiness and fulfillment, you must venture beyond living with passion and discover the purpose and dream you are destined to live for.

Living With Purpose
- Knowing your purpose is what will give you meaning in life.

Living Your Dream
- Dreams lie way outside your comfort zone and usually mean taking on bigger challenges than ever before.
- Living your dream is where the deepest level of happiness and the truest sense of fulfillment are found.

Discovering Your Purpose and Dream
- Focus on the finish line—what do you want to be remembered for?
- Focus on defining moments—moments that overwhelm you with positive emotions are pure insights into your purpose and dream.
- Focus on convenient coincidences—they are your guideposts to your dream. Become in tune with them and you will stay on course.

The Journey to Your Dream
- Stop People—these people will get in your way and attempt to stop you. Don't let them.
- Surviving The Cold—you must survive the tough times and the long bouts of no progress. This is The Cold.
- Avalanches—these are the roadblocks that will attempt to bury your dream and push you down the mountain.

Action Laws
- Law #1—Act in contribution
- Law #2—Act as though there is a way
- Law #3—Act as though you have a choice

> Use the Action Steps to define your purpose and dream and to kick-start your journey to ultimate fulfillment.

ACTION STEPS

Online version available in *The Focus Zone* at:
www.focusedstudent.com

Focus on the Finish Line

Defining Moments and Convenient Coincidences

Rapid-Fire Discovery

Your Purpose and Dream Statement

Focus on the Finish Line

Think about your departure from this planet.

1. What do you want people to remember you for?

2. What do you want people to say about you?

3. What do you want to be known for?

1.
_____

_____

2.
_____

_____

3.
_____

_____

Your Defining Moments and Convenient Coincidences

Have you had many defining moments where you caught a glimpse of your purpose or dream? Have you experienced a convenient coincidence where something amazingly helpful happened randomly? List two situations you can think of that were either a defining moment for you or a convenient coincidence. Describe them below.

1. _____

_____

_____

2. _____

_____

_____

Rapid-Fire Discovery

After reading each question, quickly jot down your thoughts in the space provided. These questions have been tested time and time again. They work wonders at uncovering your purpose and dream.

1. If you knew you couldn't fail, what would you pursue in life?

2. If you had an endless supply of money, what would you set out to achieve?

3. Who do you idolize as a hero or role model?

4. What need(s) in the world would you like to help fill?

5. What lights you up inside?

6. What would you be willing to fight for and work toward even if you didn't get paid for it?

1. _____

2. _____

3. _____

4. _____

5. _____

6. _____

Now, turn back to page 65 and review the Ambitions section of your Passion Puzzle ™. Jot down any additional ideas below.

_____

_____

Your Purpose and Dream Statement

This is where you take your first step. Use your answers from the previous three Action Steps to help complete this powerful exercise —writing a purpose and dream statement.

> *A journey of a thousand miles begins*
> *with a single step.*
>
> —Lao Tzu

Your Purpose Statement—this doesn't need to be eloquently defined, as you will continue to refine it throughout your journey. Jot down some ideas. Start with a few words and then try linking them together. (Example: to help preserve the environment.)

_____

_____

Your Dream Statement—for some people defining their dream is easier than their purpose, and for others the opposite is true. Your dream is a large project or a conquest that stems from your purpose. (Example: to help power the world using alternative energy sources that do not cause pollution.)

_____

_____

_____

_____

Congratulations! You have taken the first step in making your dream come true. Read this statement every day—post it on your wall, in your shower or make it a screen saver on your computer. Visualizing this dream—focusing on it—is the most powerful thing you can do to help it unfold.

As you continue forward through college and into your career, continue to refine and refer to your purpose and your dream statements. They will guide you in your decisions and keep you focused on living a life of ultimate fulfillment.

To create your own Dream Manifesto—a powerful way to articulate and visualize your dream—go to _The Focused Zone_ at _www.focusedstudent.com_. You will find this powerful activity in the online Action Steps.

FINAL WORDS

Your Future is in Your Hands

Twenty years from now you will be
more disappointed by the things that
you didn't do than by the ones you did do.
So throw off the bowlines.
Sail away from the safe harbor.
Catch the trade winds in your sails.

Explore. Dream. Discover.

—Mark Twain

Congratulations, you're almost at the end . . . only a few more pages to go. We know how rewarding it can be to read a book from cover to cover (especially while in college), so give yourself a pat on the back. And give yourself an even bigger pat on the back if you completed the Action Steps along the way. Although our journey together is coming to an end, things for you are just getting started.

The decisions—small and large—you make over the next few years will play a major role in shaping your future. Go after what you really want. Your future is in *your* hands— not in the hands of your professors, friends or even your well-meaning parents.

What will it be?

- **Will you adopt** an experience-focused mindset and create an amazing foundation of skills and experiences?

- **Will you determine** what gives you passion and custom-design a career in the best direction for you?

- **Will you develop** meaningful relationships with people who share your ambitions and support your dreams?

All the tools you need to build an amazing and fulfilling future are at your fingertips—literally. The question is, what will you do with them?

A home builder who doesn't use his tools to hammer a single nail will never see his blueprint turn into a beautiful home. The same is true for your life. Throughout this book we've helped you create a blueprint and we've given you the tools. Now it's up to you to start swinging the hammer!

We have seen too many friends and peers just drift through college and end up in jobs that become a meaningless routine. We don't want you to experience the same disappointment. You deserve the excitement and satisfaction that comes with a meaningful career. Don't settle for anything less. You are destined for great things—we truly believe that. There is a dream inside you waiting to be fulfilled. So let your light shine and focus on the future that you alone were born to live.

Be aware that procrastination, comfort and fear will attempt to rob you of your dreams. Every day, be on the alert—slam the door on these ruthless dream stealers! Only you can fight for the future you want—so keep your guard up, stay focused and, above all, persist.

As you might remember from middle school, Newton's first law states that an object in motion tends to stay in motion and an object at rest tends to stay at rest. So put yourself in motion and get momentum on your side. Do something every day that will move you closer to the future you really want. By continuing to take action, your momentum will build and eventually you will become unstoppable!

All you need to do now is take the first step.

Best of success!

P.S.—We packed *The Focus Zone* at www.focusedstudent.com with tools and resources to support you on your journey. This online community will remain available to you, so keep checking in to find more ways to accelerate your progress.

P.P.S.—We love to hear success stories from students, so please send yours to: success@focusedstudent.com

The Power of Focus for College Students

— Marketing Rep Opportunity —

Do you want to make BIG BUCKS sharing this book with your classmates?

We are looking for a few student leaders in each region of the continent. Selected students will join the Focused Student team as Marketing Reps and use creative strategies to distribute *The Power of Focus for College Students* within their college and community. For example:

- have your school purchase books for all incoming freshman

- help a club on campus sell the book as a fundraiser

- find a corporate sponsor to gift free copies of the book to students attending a conference

The options are endless and so is the profit potential. We are looking for student leaders who have excellent communication skills and connections on their campus. If **you** fit this profile and are looking for a part-time opportunity to make extra money, then visit:

www.focusedstudent.com/CampusRep

Want Multiple Copies of this Book?

Contact us to find out more about volume discounts and how you can use *The Power of Focus for College Students* as a marketing tool for your business or as a revenue generator for your student club or conference. It is great for graduating high school seniors, event giveaways, freshman introduction packages, corporate sponsor gifts and much more.

To inquire, call 1.888.607.6910
or send an email to
info@focusedstudent.com.

Care to be Entertained and Inspired?

Have Andrew & Luc speak at your high school, college or university

Share the focusing strategies you have learned in this book with your peers through a fun, dynamic and energizing speech. Find out how by contacting:
1-888-607-6910   info@focusedstudent.com
www.focusedstudent.com/speaking

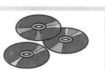

Plug in your Headphones & Learn by Listening

Get The Power of Focus for College Students audio products

- Learn new focusing strategies while you work out
- Listen to the book on your drive to school

For details, check out www.focusedstudent.com/products

Accelerate Your Progress with The Power of Focus

EXECUTIVE COACHING PROGRAM   by Les Hewitt
This is a hands-on, two-year program consisting of 12 full-day workshops for business leaders and entrepreneurs.

CORPORATE COACHING PROGRAM   by Les Hewitt
A customized one-year program for key people, conducted in-house or offsite.

WOMEN'S WORKSHOP   by Fran Hewitt
This action-packed three-day experience will help you live life fully and open your heart to what's really important.

All of these programs FOCUS on results!

For more information, dates and locations please call:

Toll Free: 1-877-678-0234
Phone: 403-295-0500

e-mail: info@thepoweroffocus.ca
www.thepoweroffocus.ca

TELL YOUR PARENTS ABOUT
The Power *of* FOCUS

RESOURCE GUIDE

The following are books and resources we feel are a great complement to a college education. Look for an asterisk* for our top six picks.

COOL COLLEGE READS

Major in Success, by Patrick Combs
Chicken Soup for the College Soul, by Jack Canfield, Mark Victor Hansen, Kimberly Kirberger, and Dan Clark
The 7 habits of Highly Effective Teens, by Sean Covey
What Should I Do With My Life?, by Po Bronson
Better Grades in Less Time, by Gary Tuerack
Rudy's Insights for Winning in Life, by Rudy Ruettiger

CAREER FOCUSING BOOKS

What Color Is Your Parachute?, by Richard Bolles
The Everything Resume Book, by Burt Nadler
The Everything Cover Letter Book, by Burt Nadler
Great Big Book of Personal Productivity, by Ron Fry

BOOKS TO HELP YOU PURSUE YOUR DREAM

The Alchemist, by Paulo Coelho
The Dream Giver, by Bruce Wilkinson
The On-purpose Person, by Kevin W. McCarthy
Atlas Shrugged, by Ayn Rand

SELF-DEVELOPMENT GREATEST HITS

The Power of Focus, by Les Hewitt, Jack Canfield, and Mark Victor Hansen
The Power of Focus for Women, by Les Hewitt and Fran Hewitt
Trump: The Art of the Deal, by Donald J. Trump
Trump: Think Like a Billionaire, by Donald J. Trump
The Success Principles, by Jack Canfield
The Aladdin Factor, by Jack Canfield and Mark Victor Hansen
The Magic of Thinking Big, by David Schwartz

The 7 Habits of Highly Effective People, by Stephen R. Covey
Dig Your Well Before You're Thirsty, by Harvey MacKay
How to Win Friends and Influence People, by Dale Carnegie
Leading an Inspired Life, by Jim Rohn
Feel the Fear and Do It Anyway, by Susan Jeffers
Even Eagles Need a Push, by David McNally
Your Life Only a Gazillion Times Better, by Cathy Breslin and Judy May Murphy
Networking Magic, by Jill Lublin and Rick Frishman

BECOMING WEALTHY

The Automatic Millionaire, by David Bach
Rich Dad, Poor Dad, by Robert Kiyosaki
Cashflow Quadrant, by Robert Kiyosaki
Retire Young, Retire Rich, by Robert Kiyosaki
Secrets of the Millionaire Mind, by T. Harv Eker
The Wealthy Barber, by David Chilton
Trump: How to Get Rich, by Donald J. Trump
Think and Grow Rich, by Napoleon Hill
Getting Loaded: Make a Million . . . While You're Still Young Enough to Enjoy It,
    by Peter G. Bielagus
Cracking the Millionaire Code, by Mark Victor Hansen and Robert Allen
Real Estate Riches, by Dolf de Roos
Real Estate Investing in Canada, by Don R. Campbell

OTHER GREAT READS

The Power of Faithful Focus, by Les Hewitt and Dr. Charlie Self
Chicken Soup for the Soul, by Jack Canfield and Mark Victor Hansen
The Power of Now, by Eckhart Tolle
Jump In!, by Mark Burnett
The Celestine Prophecy, by James Redfield
Forever Young: Ten Gifts of Faith for the Graduate, by Pat Williams
From Good to Great, by Jim Collins
The Artists' Way, by Julia Cameron
Body for Life, by Bill Phillips

AUDIO-BOOKS

Any book that is worth listening to (and more) is available at
www.audible.com. Just download and go!

**For a great guide of websites to help you in college go to
www.focusedstudent.com/resources**

ABOUT THE AUTHORS

 **Andrew Hewitt** took a unique approach to college that earned him much more than a bachelor of management degree. As a student he studied and worked in the United States, Canada, Europe and Asia—visiting over 30 cities across 13 countries. Among other initiatives, he competed internationally in entrepreneurship competitions, facilitated nationwide student leader conferences, and founded and led a number of student clubs. As a result of his focused approach to college, Andrew was featured in national publications, received several prominent awards and became a target for corporate recruiters. Rather than graduate into a comffy six-figure corporate job, Andrew pursued his passion for helping students.

As the son of two professional speakers, he was well equipped for the personal development industry and his work quickly caught the attention of New York Billionaire Donald Trump. He now works with Trump University and is the co-creator of their home study program *Start Right! How to Launch a Great Career.* In addition to being a passionate speaker and a trained Dream Discovery Coach, Andrew serves on the board of the Canadian Business School Council and is an accomplished real estate investor.

His mission is to help induce a massive change in the way students are educated, so that it becomes common practice to equip and empower students to live life fully and to pursue their dreams.

To get in touch with Andrew, e-mail him at:
andrew@focusedstudent.com

 **Luc d'Abadie** travels the continent alongside his business partner, Andrew Hewitt, with the mission of helping students discover and reach their full potential. Luc graduated with an honors degree in math and business from the University of Waterloo. A few of his many college experiences include starting two well-known professional development clubs, being awarded multiple scholarships, competing in international business plan competitions and selling BlackBerry® handhelds in Europe to Fortune 500 companies. He has also been featured in newspapers and magazines across North America, including the *Chicago Tribune, Denver Post, Detroit Free Press, Calgary Herald* and *Canadian Business Magazine* for his entrepreneurial achievements and networking creativity.

In 2005 the star of *The Apprentice,* Donald Trump, noticed Luc's passion for equipping students with the success principles they need to get ahead. Luc has since joined the Trump University team and is the co-creator of their audio program *Start Right! How to Launch a Great Career.* His love for writing extends beyond this book. He has also written a novel and distributes an inspiration e-column to subscribers in over nine countries. Luc spends the majority of his time sharing *The Power of Focus for College Students* principles with students around the world through summer programs, one-on-one dream coaching, and speaking as a youth motivator on the college circuit.

To contact Luc, send him an email at:
luc.d@focusedstudent.com

Les Hewitt, originally from Northern Ireland, is a top performance coach and founder of *The Power of Focus Inc.* The company provides top-quality personal development products and services to individuals and companies in Canada, the United States, Australia, and Ireland.

Since its inception in 1983, *The Power of Focus Inc.* (formerly *Achievers Canada)* has created and promoted more than 900 workshops and seminars for thousands of businesspeople from a wide variety of industries.

Les is a dynamic speaker, business coach, sales trainer, writer and entrepreneur. For the past twenty years he has coached hundreds of entrepreneurs to achieve exceptional results.

His first book, *The Power of Focus,* is an international best-seller, having sold more than half a million copies in North America to date. It has been translated into nineteen languages. Other titles he has co-authored are *The Power of Focus for Women* with his wife, Fran, and *The Power of Faithful Focus* with Dr. Charlie Self.

To contact Les, or obtain information about *The Power of Focus* coaching programs, licensing partnership opportunities, speeches or workshops contact:

THE POWER OF FOCUS INC.
Suite 220, 2421 – 37th Avenue NE
Calgary, Alberta, Canada T2E 6Y7

toll free: 877-678-0234 / ph: 403-295-0500
fax: 403-730-4548
website: www.thepoweroffocus.ca
email: info@thepoweroffocus.ca